Praise for *Everywhere God*

Knowing Alicia personally
hearing hear speak, I expected *Everywhere God to be* ....
and honest. She certainly didn't disappoint me and I know her
readers will not be disappointed either. Alicia wonderfully and
articulately examines the thread of God's presence which she
explains is woven into every aspect of our lives and into the
fabric of of the world around us. Everywhere weaves together
deeper theological truths, Alicia's own story and practical ad-
vise into a seamless must-read for any Christian woman wanting to see God everywhere.
Amy Spiegel
Author of *Letting Go of Perfect*

In *Everywhere God*, Alicia Brummeler delivers the nourishment
we all need: a feast of spiritual meaning. She draws it not from
faraway abstractions, but from the concrete corners of our daily lives—the workplace, the home, the garden. This practical,
insightful book is perfect for book groups, small groups, and individual readers who are hungry to find God's sacred presence
in the ordinary.
Andrea Palpant Dilley
Contributor editor for *Christianity Today*

For a younger generation of people who seek to unite the parts
of life once defined as sacred versus secular, *Everywhere God* examines this dichotomy and encounters God in all parts of life.
From parenting to the workplace the author's journey takes us
deep into everyday life where we find God present on every
level. A great strength of this book are the questions and outstanding resources at the end of each chapter that invite readers
into further discussion and reflection.
Margie Haack
Author of *The Exact Place* and *God in the Sink*

I came away from reading *Everywhere God* feeling as if I had just spent time with a wise and spirited friend. Alicia Brummeler invites us to come along with her, seeing everything and every place as an opportunity to meet God. If you want to develop more intention and attentiveness in your life, this book is for you.

Nancy Nordenson
Author of *Finding Livelihood: A Progress of Work and Leisure* and *Just Think: Nourish Your Mind to Feed Your Soul.*

Alicia Brummeler declares that "real life doesn't have spiritual revival weeks," and how true she is. However within the pages of *Everywhere God*, Alicia provides an opportunity to experience a spiritual awakening in the ordinary parts of everyday life. Her stories heighten sensitivities to the mundane with an invitation to look at life through the lens of faith. It teases the heart, poking at the old to see God in a new way, new setting, and with new purpose, while promising that He is, indeed, everywhere.

Elisa Pulliam
Author of *Meet the New You*
Founder of MoretoBe.com

Everywhere God

Exploring the Ordinary Places

Tina —

So glad our paths crossed again! May you encounter our everywhere God in these pages.

♡ Alicia

Everywhere God: Exploring the Ordinary Places
Published by:

Kalos Press—an imprint of Doulos Resources, 195 Mack Edwards Drive, Oakland, TN 38060; PHONE: (901) 201-4612 WEBSITES: www.kalospress.org; www.doulosresources. org.

Please address all questions about rights and reproduction to Doulos Resources: PHONE: (901) 201-4612; E-MAIL: info@doulosresources.org.

Published 2016

Printed in the United States of America by Ingram/Lightning Source

Colophon:

Cover design by Robyn Clark; interior design by Julie Hollyday.

Copyediting by Lydia Tisdale; proofreading help provided by: Nathalia Kane & Paige Landino.

Typefaces include Baskerville (body text set in 11pt.); Neutra Text, and Thank You Slanted.

This book is printed using [50lb. 444 ppi "crème" archival paper] that is produced according to Sustainable Forestry Initiative® (SFI®) Certified Sourcing.

Brummeler, Alicia, 1970–
      Everywhere God: Exploring the Ordinary Places.
ISBNs: 978-1-937063-38-2 (print); 978-1-937063-37-5 (digital)
                   2016958678

13 14 15 16 17 18 19 20   10 9 8 7 6 5 4 3 2 1

For Brad, Jacob, and Anna—with love and thanks. These stories are not just mine, but yours as well.

Contents

A Beginning

So here's what I want you to do, God helping you: Take your everyday, ordinary life—
your sleeping, eating, going-to-work, and
walking-around life—and place it before
God as an offering.

—Romans 12:1 (The Message)

I was 20 when I married. I knew I loved my husband and
God, but I knew very little about myself. Like many young
adults, my twenties were growing years. Suddenly, I was figuring out how to manage a household, work a full-time job,
grocery shop and budget, be a wife, daughter-in-law, eventual
mother, and, oh yes, grow closer to God too. I wanted more
to my spiritual life than weekly church services and a smat-
tering of Bible reading and prayer. Something was missing,
but I still couldn't conceptualize my spiritual life as anything
but another item on my to-do list. Daily devotions—check.
Attend church—check. Bring snack to small group—check.
There was spiritual growth in one compartment, and then
there was the rest of my life. The part of me that worked a
full-time job, navigated married life, and cooked dinner each
night felt more like the "real" me. Was this how "grown-up"

faith looked? Did I need to adjust my expectations?

My childhood was happy and looked "normal," but I certainly had some bizarre, irrational fears. After watching an episode of *The A-Team* in which a motorcycle gang takes over a small town, I was convinced that every motorcycle rider was out to take over *my* small town too. Once, on a long car trip, I saw a group of motorcycle riders on the road. I crouched down in the back seat of our car, thinking that if they couldn't see me they wouldn't hurt me or my family. Though now I laugh at my silly fears, they were a real part of my childhood and they left their mark on my impressionable mind. As a child, I also feared dying and going to hell and it was this fear that prompted me, in part, to faith. I remember sitting in my mom's lap and hearing the news that I did not have to dread death or hell because of what Jesus had done for me. Together we prayed and I accepted Jesus as my Savior. A sense of peace and relief washed over me that night as I fell asleep.

Though I remember deciding to trust in Jesus, I can't remember a time when I wasn't a Christian. I attended Sunday school and Vacation Bible School as a young child, and youth group and church camp as a teenager, growing in knowledge and in faith. When I became a student at Taylor University, my favorite weeks of the year were Spiritual Renewal Weeks. During those chapel services and evening sessions I prayed earnestly for a "God encounter." I depended on the spiritual highs to carry me through the rest of the semester.

It wasn't until my twenties, as a newlywed and a young, working woman that I began to wonder why my spiritual life felt segmented: sacred on the one side, secular on the other side.

Real life didn't have Spiritual Renewal Weeks.

This realization made me disappointed and even a bit fearful. Being an adult didn't look nearly as inviting as it used to. How was I to bring together these two parts of my life— my faith and everything else? I couldn't shake the niggling sense that there was more to the Christian life than weekly small group and church attendance. But I didn't see a way forward. If you had asked me, "List the ways a person can experience God's presence," reading a novel or working in the yard would *not* have occurred to me. My list would have included activities like going to church or participating in a Bible study because that was all I knew. How relieved I was to find that I was wrong! Little did I know that in small, barely discernible ways, my journey towards encountering God in the everyday was about to begin. Looking back, I realize that while I heard "all truth is God's truth" in church and at university, it had not yet moved from an intellectual understanding to a tangible reality in my life.

Early in my marriage, while I was living in Illinois, my mom handed me a copy of Edith Schaeffer's *The Hidden Art of Homemaking*.[1] "You will enjoy reading this," Mom said. She was right. The idea of "hidden art"—art which is found in the minor (ordinary) areas of life—resonated deeply with me. By the time I read Schaeffer's book, in the mid 1990s, some parts were dated and even a bit quaint, but that didn't deter me from hearing her message. *Encountering God in my everyday*

life can begin at home? You mean stopping to notice a flower and appreciating its beauty can be an act of worship? This was new territory for me. Edith Schaeffer seamlessly integrated her faith into all areas of her life and this delighted me. She wrote about eating, gardening, walking, cooking, talking, and God all in the same mix. I loved it! Schaeffer's writings gave me the permission I needed to think differently about my relationship with God, creation, and the ordinary parts of my life. I began to read others—Kathleen Norris, Wendell Berry, Eugene Peterson, and Dennis and Margie Haack—and to engage in conversations with friends who were living lives that integrated their everyday routines with their faith.

Twenty-some years later, I am still on my journey. My "sleeping, eating, going-to-work, and walking-around life" continues to discover God's active and real presence in my everyday life. This book is the story of that journey and what I have learned along the way. Maybe my stories will resonate deeply, and you'll find yourself saying, "Me too!" Or maybe something I say will simply light a spark and you will discover ways to encounter God that look different from the ways that worked for me. One thing is certain: God reveals himself to each of us, often in surprising ways.

HOW TO READ THIS BOOK

This book is arranged topically, with each chapter divided into three sections. In the first section, I provide a definition and biblical framework for the topic. In the second section, I discuss why this topic is important. In the third section, I outline ways a person can encounter God, with practical suggestions and ideas. Though I recommend that you begin with chapter one, *Encountering God in Creation*, feel free to jump around and read the chapters in a way that suits you. At the end of each chapter, I provide questions for further reflection, along with additional reading resources. My hope is that you will find yourself coming back to this book again and again, underlining and marking passages as you continue to encounter our everywhere God in your ordinary moments.

Encountering God in Creation

Look at the stars! look, look up at the skies
O look at all the fire-folk sitting in the air!
—Gerard Manley Hopkins, "The Starlight
Night"[2]

I felt my breath catch in my throat. Below me, the city lights of Vancouver twinkled in the distance. The night air was crisp and cold. Above me, an explosion of stars scattered the nighttime sky. On either side of me, tall pine trees lined the ski slope. I couldn't believe I was in this place, at this particular moment. How did a Midwest girl from Indiana end up in Vancouver, British Columbia, skiing with her husband and children on a Saturday night? Never in my wildest dreams did I imagine that we could afford ski passes while Brad attended graduate school. But the ski mountain offered an incredible deal for season passes and Vancouver boasted a large number of consignment ski shops, and so we managed, this once, to squeeze skiing into our budget.

So here we were. Having the time of our lives. Pausing for a moment before heading down the run, I thanked God for his creation and this experience—for the brilliant stars and for the cold, pristine air. A part of me recognized that this was a sacred moment and I wanted to sear the image of the surrounding beauty into my mind so that I would never forget it.

Since that time, I have recalled that moment often. I encountered God that night on Grouse Mountain—in the crispness of the nighttime air, in the starry show overhead, and in the majestic pine trees surrounding me. The beauty and grandeur of that place filled me with praise and adoration for my Creator.

CREATION: WHAT IS IT?

All stories begin somewhere. For me, the creation story began with a sky blue flannel-graph board in Sunday school. Seated in a circle with my other Sunday school friends, I watched the story unfold. From an empty board, to the addition of a sun and a moon, to trees and flowers, to animals and Adam and Eve, I recognized that creation was the living, growing things all around me, created by the God of the universe. The zucchini, tomato, and cucumber plants that my parents planted in their garden each summer—God created them. The fig and pomegranate trees growing in my grandparent's backyard—God created them. The Bluegill fish I caught in the pond beside my house—God created them.

It was in this same Sunday school circle that I learned about creation's brokenness too. As a result of Adam and Eve's disobedience in the garden, sin entered the picture, affecting the entire created realm. Later in the Sunday school year, I learned about Jesus, the Messiah, and realized the creation story wasn't finished. Some day Christ would return and restore creation, making all things new. Not only that, but Christ would dwell with his people for all eternity.

As I advanced beyond the flannel-graph story of creation and grew into adulthood, Paul's words in Romans 8:22–23, where he says we long and groan for the redemption of our bodies and creation, echoed my own experience, my own body. From stretch marks to brown spots to a bum left big toe, my physical body reflects brokenness, minimal as it may be. As I matured and paid more attention to the world around me, I saw creation at large suffering too.

The headlines constantly remind us of the fragile state of God's creation. From droughts to fires, from hurricanes to floods, everything experiences the effects of the Fall. But rather than despair over this situation, there is hope: Christ promises us a new creation someday. In Revelation 21, John tells us, "Then I saw a new heaven and a new earth, for the first heaven and the first earth had passed away….'the dwelling place of God is with man. He will dwell with them.'" It will be a perfect creation.

CREATION: WHY IS IT IMPORTANT?

Why does this understanding of creation matter? Think of how we build relationships. We don't start by sharing our deepest longings with another person. We start by learning a bit about the other person. *Where are you from? What do you do? How do you spend your free time?* These "basics" lay the foundation for the relationship. Over time, we learn more. *Who has had the most impact on your life? What makes you afraid? What are your dreams?* Every time we walk out the door or look out the window we see some element of creation—a bird, a flower, a tree, a bit of grass. Creation is one of the most obvious things to notice about God. This recognition serves as a starting point for deepening our relationship with Christ and reveals attributes of God's character.

CREATION EXEMPLIFIES ORDER AND BEAUTY

When my children were little and they wanted to paint, I had to overcome the part of myself that didn't like messes. However, watching them excitedly jump up and down as they planned their next "masterpiece," quickly put my "neat-mom self" in her proper place. As toddlers, their "masterpieces" often turned into brown blobs because they tried to mix too many colors together. As they grew and their fine-motor skills developed, real pictures emerged, showcasing brightly-colored birds, sharks, and houses. This desire to create and to place objects in a specific place—"Mommy, I want the sun to go *here*"—speaks to the fact that we are made in God's image. We reflect his attributes, including a desire for order and beauty. Read chapters 1 and 2 of Genesis and notice the way in which God creates. Day one: God creates the day and night. Day two: God separates the water from the sky. Each day follows an orderly progression. And creation isn't just orderly; it's beautiful. When God creates trees, the text specifically says these were trees that were pleasant to the sight (Gen. 2:9). God's "masterpiece," his created world, reflects order and beauty. This is a creation that never grows stale or outdated. Whether we are in our 30s or 80s, we continue to marvel at its beauty.

CREATION FOLLOWS A RHYTHM

For most of my life, I have lived in places with four discernible seasons. Fall is my favorite, but as each season draws to a close,

I find myself anticipating the next one. Each season contains some unique and delightful aspect. Spring means bulb flowers and asparagus; summer means basil and *al fresco* dining; fall means pumpkins and sweaters; winter means hearty stews and fires in the fireplace. Creation follows a rhythm, even in climates without noticeable seasons. The writer of Ecclesiastes says, "The sun rises, and the sun goes down, and hastens to the place where it rises. The wind blows to the south and goes around to the north; around and around goes the wind, and on its circuits the wind returns" (1:4–6).

Sometimes, the rhythms of creation surprise, even devastate us. In the fall of 2012, Hurricane Sandy swept across the northeastern seaboard of the United States, bringing terrible destruction. Power lines snapped like twigs, huge trees crashed to the ground, and hundreds of thousands of homes lost electricity and experienced flooding. And this was the second hurricane to hit our area within 15 months. In order to maintain a positive attitude, I told my family we would live like Laura Ingalls Wilder and her family in the 1800s. We rose with the sun each morning and went to bed when it was dark. We built fires in our fireplace to keep warm (we were fortunate to have another source of heat as many homes in our neighborhood were cold *and* dark). Slowly, we adjusted to having more darkness in the house than light. When our power was eventually restored and I could easily light a room with a flip of a switch or make my morning coffee with the press of a button, I still couldn't forget the rhythms of work and rest, day and night. The option of staying up late checking emails or working at the computer simply hadn't been a possibility the week before.

Don't get me wrong. I am grateful for the many creature comforts this era affords. Yet at times, I wonder if this constant access to electricity and technology limits our ability to recognize the God-given rhythms that allow space both for work and for rest.

GOD COMMUNICATES THROUGH CREATION

Long before my "Grouse Mountain" moment, I was aware of God's presence in creation. As a young girl, standing next to the enormous Sequoia trees in northern California, I recognized that something bigger than myself created these massive redwoods. This "largeness" of God filled me with awe and praise. Rather than feeling intimidated or frightened, I felt God's presence. It was so clear to me that I could never fashion something this grand. I also experienced God's delight standing next to those trees. He took pleasure in my enjoyment of his creation.

On a daily basis, God's personal nature is revealed to us in myriad ways through his created world. From cardinals at the birdfeeder to pink-hued sunsets, from rushing waterfalls to flower-filled meadows, we see examples of a creative and lavish God. Such colors! Such beauty! The Psalms do a wonderful job of reminding us of this truth. Psalm 19 begins, *"The heavens declare the glory of God; and the sky above proclaims his handiwork. Day to day pours out speech, and night to night reveals knowledge. There is no speech, nor are there words, whose voice is not heard"* (vv. 1–4). If we look and pay attention, we discover God communicating his creativity, his care, and his love to us through his creation.

CREATION ENCOURAGES THE HABIT OF ATTENTION

It is not easy to pay attention to the natural world. Our lives are busy and often we are distracted by the competing demands on our time. But cultivating the habit of attention is necessary to appreciate creation. How often do you pause in the morning when the sun is rising, thanking God for making the beautiful sunrise and giving you a new day? When was the last time you stopped to watch a bird perched on a tree branch, reminding yourself of God's care for the bird and also of his care for you? Or when was the last time you really smelled a flower and enjoyed its beautiful fragrance? When we are attentive, we can encounter God in those small moments. God speaks to us through creation when we stop, look, and listen. The next time you witness a stunning sunset or a picturesque view, pause, even if it is just for a minute. The Psalmist encourages us to "be still and know that I am God" (Ps 46:10). Quiet your heart and mind. Embrace the silence. Before you move onto the next task, thank God for whatever it is that caught your attention. This may feel forced or awkward at first, but gradually you find that a new habit has developed. One that feels unforced and natural.

GOD MEETS US IN CREATION—EVEN IN THE DARK MOMENTS

Sometimes in our darkest moments, sometimes in our merely dismal points of gloom, God meets us in creation. I already mentioned that my family lived in Vancouver, BC, for a period of time. We moved there at the end of 2003 so Brad could attend graduate school at Regent College. He was thirty-five, I was thirty-three, and our two children were seven and four. Going to graduate school at this point in our lives, along with moving our family across the continent, was a big deal. Even bigger was the fact that our house in Elgin, Illinois, still had not sold at the time of our move. In spite of the anxious questions (*what if we can't pay our bills?*) that floated in and out of our thoughts and the finite amount of dollars in our savings account, we felt God wanted us to continue with our plans and to trust him for our financial situation. Our house had already been on the market for three months—surely it would sell soon!

Two blocks from our rental house was a golf course with a beautiful tree-covered walking path. Most days of the week I would walk my laps, praying for our house to sell. There was a certain section of the path where the trees separated and, on a clear day, I would have an amazing view of the coastal mountains. For most of the year, the tops of the mountains were also snow-covered. Whenever I saw that view, Psalm 121 came to mind: "I lift up my eyes to the hills. From where does my help come? My help comes from the Lord, who made heaven and earth." Five months after moving, our house finally sold. I spent many a day worried and filled with anxiety about our financial situation, but during those moments on my walks, I encountered God and felt his peace and presence in my life. It was as if he were saying to me, "Don't worry, Alicia, I have it under control. After all, I made the heavens and the earth!"

UNDERSTANDING CREATION PROMPTS US TO BETTER CARE FOR IT

Lastly, creation matters because God has made us stewards over his created realm, which he alone rules, promotes, and blesses. The more alert we are to his creation, the more we realize it needs better care. This can be a touchy subject because of the strong opinions people have about environmentalism. It's like talking about religion and politics at the dinner table—beware! However, many faithful Christians are concerned about the environment and take this responsibility very seriously. Perhaps considering care for creation in terms of tending God's world rather than in terms of environmentalism is a more helpful way to think.

A number of years ago, I discovered an excellent book called *Caring for Creation in Your Own Backyard* by Loren and Mary Ruth Wilkinson. Loren is a retired professor at Regent College and Mary Ruth taught as a seasonal lecturer there. They give a wonderful explanation for why *earthkeeping* (their term) is important. The book is arranged by seasons and each section is filled with practical ideas on how to protect and use the earth's resources wisely along with ways a person can do this in his or her own home. The Wilkinsons use the term earthkeeping because it suggests "not only the everydayness of 'housekeeping' but also the breadth of our larger home, the whole created earth."[3] As Christians, our concern should not only be for our homes but also for the created world that God made, the surrounding spaces we inhabit and the communities in which we live. Instead of trying to "save the planet" (an overwhelming and daunting task!), we can begin caring for creation in our homes and communities, taking each day as a gift from our loving Creator.

CREATION: WAYS WE CAN ENCOUNTER GOD

Encountering God in creation begins in a backyard, on a porch, or on a balcony. One of the chapters in *The Hidden Art of Homemaking* states very plainly, "we all live somewhere."[4] It may be a house with a backyard, an apartment, a dorm

room, a room in your parent's house, a cottage, or even a
cave! We have a place we call home. It is in this place that we
can begin to experience God through creation.

BRING CREATION INSIDE

An easy first step is to bring plants, flowers, or both, into
your home. If it is a plant, as you water it and care for it,
thank God for creating this particular plant. Thank him for
the beauty and intricacy of the plant. Admit to him that you
could not create such a thing or make it grow. Depending on
how far you want to go with this, you could go online and
learn about your particular plant species. Do you know its
scientific name? Do you recognize the type of leaf it has? Do
you know what kind of climate it prefers? In knowing some-
thing, just like in knowing some*one*, we feel a stronger affini-
ty for that particular thing. By studying the complex details
of a particular plant, you also learn about the grandeur of
the Creator. When we notice creation, we catch glimpses of
artistry, originality, and beauty, in addition to structure and
form.

Perhaps houseplants are not your thing. You can still find
ways to bring creation into your home. For instance, shells—
no watering or sunlight required. If you have ever walked
along the beach, you know the variety of shells to be found. I
have a collection from all the beaches I have visited over the
years. What about pieces of driftwood or unique rocks? God
created these too and they can be reminders of his creativity and variety of creation. As you look at them, notice the
details and talk to God during this time. Thank him for the
starfish, the smooth stone, and the weather-beaten piece of
driftwood. Remember the travels and the meaningful times

with friends or family members that were a part of the experience when you collected the objects.

I alluded to flowers a moment ago, and I have to say our European friends get this one right. Fresh flowers are a daily part of their lives, not a luxury or only for marking a milestone event. The habit of buying or gathering fresh flowers provides seasonal beauty and a subtle fragrance to homes. There have been times when I felt like I couldn't spend the extra ten dollars for a bouquet of flowers when money was tight. So that week I might use fresh fruit to bring color to my table or cut a branch from a shrub or a tree, creating a budget-friendly arrangement. If you are protesting "I'm just not the creative type," that's okay. I don't consider myself an artistic person. However, I can copy others' ideas. If I see an idea on Pinterest or in a magazine, I try to mimic it, even if I don't have the exact materials on hand. If you feel you don't have the time or the energy to scour Pinterest or magazines for ideas, you can start by placing a bowl of seasonal fresh fruit on the table or putting pinecones in a basket. If you have children, enlist their help. Make it a game to find five pieces of creation to bring inside. "Ohh" and "Ahh" over each discovery. Just because we may not have a natural inclination towards design, we can practice humility and joy when we bring creation inside, even if the arrangement is lopsided or sparse. God is the ultimate designer and creator. Our humble efforts are opportunities to thank our heavenly Father for his love and creativity.

PLANT A GARDEN

Do you want to do a little more? Plant a garden. If you aren't sure how to begin, at the end of this chapter I recommend some websites and books that will inspire and instruct.

You may be surprised to find how much the act of gardening parallels the care of our spiritual lives! Our souls need tending just like our gardens. If we allow the weeds to grow, we must pull them out. Sometimes this is painful, hard work. Our souls can experience moments of growth and drought just like our gardens. Working in the soil can be therapeutic too—in fact, I like to call gardening free therapy! As I plant or tend, I have the time and the space to mull over concerns or ideas. Gardening also provides a sense of accomplishment as plants grow and produce and container gardening is a perfect way to experiment. You can grow vegetables, herbs, flowers, or all three in pots! If you have a plot of earth, a porch, or a window sill, you can plant a garden.

I still feel like a novice gardener in many ways. I've had my share of victories and defeats. When our family lived in Central Texas, I loved the opportunity of having two growing seasons. For my first winter garden I planted onions, broccoli, and Brussels sprouts. When the first green shoots of my onion bulbs poked through the soil, I could barely contain my excitement. It made me want to dance around my garden! They were growing! In my spring garden, I watched lettuces, tomatoes, and cucumbers thrive before the onslaught of intense summer heat.

I also know the frustration of watching a plant shrivel up literally overnight. When we lived in Illinois, I could never get zucchini to grow. One moment I would have a beautiful, robust plant, and the next day (truly!) the plant would be withered and dead. I tried to grow zucchini in two different years and was unsuccessful both times. Now I am afraid to grow zucchini. How much more like real life can gardening get? We become afraid to keep trying something after repeated failures. Gardening exposes our finitude in ways that are good for us. We live in a culture that tries to convince us we can control everything—our careers, our marriage, our children. Gardens have a way of showing us our limitations.

In addition, gardens teach us to tend creation. They communicate God's care and provision for us, as beautifully illustrated in Isaiah 5. God, the ever-faithful gardener, experiences the joys and disappointments of "gardening" his chosen people.

In the simple act of planting fruits and vegetables, we are reminded of how God faithfully provides food for us. We feel a lot like parents when we garden. The vested interest we bring to our parenting we also bring to our gardening. We want our plants to do well—to thrive. And yet, sometimes they fail. We are disappointed, even angry, when the snail attacks our fledging plants.

If you have children, gardens are a wonderful way to teach them to care for creation. When my daughter Anna was younger, she became more excited than I did when new plants sprang up in the garden.

Try your hand at gardening. It may be a tomato plant in a pot or a window-sill herb garden, but start with something. You will experience God's creation in a new way as you garden, while enjoying fresh produce that is flavorful, healthy, and locally sourced.

CREATION IN THE WORKPLACE

Our workplaces can also provide opportunities to encounter God through creation. If your work involves designing or creating workplaces, don't forget about creation in the process! We aren't machines. Working in a cubicle all day with no windows does something to our souls. If you work in such an environment, bring a plant to your office or other pieces of creation to give your eye something pleasing to look at. Make it a point, when you are able, to eat lunch outside at a park. Seek out the green spaces in your area. In New York City, many skyscrapers contain gardens because architects recognize how beauty and living things affect our productivity and mental outlook. If your job entails driving, remind yourself to thank God for the changing landscape. Practice attentiveness to creation even as you drive. If you are in a position where you oversee a staff, could you ever hold a meeting outside? We spend so much of our time at work, rubbing shoulders with colleagues, sometimes in stressful situations. Finding ways to bring creation into 'the daily grind' can remind us of God's presence even in the nitty-gritty. This blesses both believers and those not yet aware of God's desire to bless.

SHARE CREATION

Creation doesn't belong to us. It is a gift. God has graciously given us his creation to enjoy and use, and we can share it with others. There are groups across the country that devote themselves to creating urban green spaces and gardens. Efforts like theirs force us to open our eyes and to extend creation to the unlovely places in our everyday lives. It helps us recognize that creation isn't ours to hold onto, and that we do not have exclusive rights to its beauty. A church we attended while living in Waco converted an empty lot to a community garden. In this poor and run-down neighborhood, the garden served a variety of needs. It provided fresh food to families in the community and it provided beauty in the midst of urban decay.

If you have visited a country where the ecosystems have

suffered from soil damage and run-off, you know what it is like to crave green grass, lush plants, and trees. These places have been deforested, and what was once a growing, thriving area is now semi-desert. As caretakers of God's creation, we have a responsibility to these places, even if they are far away from us. Believe me, writing this makes me squirm too. What can *I* do for a place thousands of miles away? To start, I can support legitimate organizations that care and promote sustainable farming and growing practices. I can purchase products that are fairly traded and benefit the local grower. I can be aware of the issues and make more informed choices as I shop. These are all doable starting points.

But you don't have to travel thousands of miles to share creation. If you have ever lived next to an avid gardener during growing season, most likely you have benefitted from some of the garden's abundance. Barbara Kingsolver, in her book *Animal, Vegetable, Miracle*, talks about zucchini this way. In her part of the country, kind neighbors have been known to leave bags of zucchini at the mailbox, on the porch, in the car. Potlucks are opportunities to create as many zucchini dishes as you can.[5] Something happens when we grow our own food that makes it almost unbearable to waste it or throw it away. We want others to use it as well. If only we felt as strongly about wasting food that we purchase in the grocery store!

Sharing creation isn't limited to garden produce. It can be bringing a single, lovely flower to a friend who is hurting or sick. It can be making a delicious meal for a family. Even taking care of the green space we own, making it pleasing to the eye, can be an act of sharing creation. Edith Schaeffer talks about creating lovely table arrangements with pieces of creation such as a pretty tree branch, some unique rocks, bits of moss, or a single flower so that when your family, roommate, or even you sit down to a meal there is something pleasing for the eye to behold. These simple touches communicate care. They say, "You matter." Or "I am glad to share this meal with you." Something happens inside us when we see artistry and know that someone took the time to create beauty for us to enjoy. I like to think of it as a God-stirring. These stirrings prompt us to thank and praise God. Creating table arrangements is also a great way to involve your kids. They love to create designs and organize items. When it was my daughter's turn to set the table, often we would find our napkins arranged in a special fashion or the candles on the table lit. I loved seeing the way Anna brought beauty to the dinner table. When we share our garden produce or some flowers with others, we recognize God's goodness. We are thankful for the abundance we have been given; we are thankful for beauty and objects that are pleasing to the eye; we are thankful that all good gifts come from God.

ENJOY CREATION

Not only can we share creation but we can also enjoy it, even during the difficult times. When the Israelites were exiled to Babylon after failing to heed God's repeated commands to repent, God gave a message to the prophet Jeremiah to pass along to his people. He tells them, "Build houses and settle down; plant gardens and eat what they produce. Marry and have sons and daughters; find wives for your sons and give your daughters in marriage, so that they too may have sons and daughters. Increase in number there; do not decrease. Also, seek the peace and prosperity of the city to which I have carried you into exile" (Jer. 29:4–7 NIV). No matter where we live, no matter what season of life we are in, we need to settle down and enjoy the place we are in. It would have been easy for the Israelites to think that real life would only begin again once they returned to the Promised Land, the Temple, and their homes. Likewise, those of us in transition, those who are stay-at-home moms, those living in less-than-ideal locations or in troublesome circumstances, need to heed Jeremiah's words. God is present wherever we live, whatever the situation. That doesn't mean we can't work for better conditions; some of our personal states may be truly awful and in need of change. But if we constantly long for the next place or the next season in life, we run the risk of missing out on what God has for us at the moment.

Our family lived in Vancouver for almost three years. While we lived there, we tried to take advantage of all the city had to offer, knowing we were there for only a set period of time. When Brad began looking at PhD programs, Baylor University caught his eye. I remember thinking, "Not Waco, Lord, please." Waco it was, and the transition was difficult for me. For starters, you could not find two more opposite places in terms of physical beauty than Vancouver and Waco. Gone was the lush greenness and temperate climate of British Columbia complete with beautiful mountain views. Instead there was a lot of brown everywhere, and six months of the year were just plain hot. Struggling to keep my grass alive made me long for the next chapter in our lives. But I didn't want to live that way. Waco was home for our family and according to Jeremiah, I needed to settle down and plant my garden.

God wants us to live in our present reality, not waiting for the next chapter. Slowly, I began to put down roots and make Waco home. I began to look for the positives in my situation, starting with the two growing seasons that I could now take advantage of. I looked for walking routes that had lovely homes and yards, which inspired me. As a family, we would regularly take day trips to Austin and I fell in love with the beauty of the Hill Country. We moved from Waco in 2011, and believe it or not, I found it hard to leave. No, I wouldn't miss the heat, the poison ivy, and the fire ants, but I had put down roots in that community and it was my home. Anytime a person is in a transitory phase of life such as being a student, it can be especially hard to make a place home, but make the effort to become familiar with where you live. Live life in the present and seek God in that place, however brief it may be.

Additionally, part of enjoying creation means you are in it. This can be hard to do at certain times of the year when the temperatures are either extremely hot or cold, but it can be done. If I wanted to walk outside during the summer months in Texas, I had to be out early in the morning. When I lived in Vancouver, I saw moms out in the rain with their children. Many had strollers outfitted with plastic covers to protect against the elements, and the mom had the appropriate rain gear. Wherever you may live, by all means take advantage of the seasons when you can be outside without a lot of hassle! Invite a friend to walk or jog with you. Hike the local trails at nearby parks, ride a bike, eat a meal outside, rent a canoe and paddle down a river, play freeze tag with your kids in the backyard. Get outside and smell the fresh air. Take time to notice the creation around you. These moments outside can also provide opportunities for prayer. Often when I walk, I find myself praying about whatever is on my mind at the moment. The pounding of my feet and the quickening of my breath push me into a cadence of prayer. Memorizing scripture or favorite passages from books seem to happen more easily while walking. In her book, *Holy is the Day*, Carolyn Weber talks about reciting poetry while she walks.[6] The prayers, the recitations, the stillness become opportunities to encounter God's presence.

You can also enjoy creation by traveling and seeing new places. I am always a little in awe of adventure hikers and travelers—especially the ones who go to a totally new place by themselves and explore it. Several years ago, I read a book about Isabella Bird, called *A Lady's Life in the Rocky Mountains*.[7] Bird was from Britain and her story tells of her adventures while exploring Estes Park and the Rocky Mountains in 1873, long before those areas were developed. The land was rugged and sparse in terms of inhabitants and suitable lodging. She traveled by herself and often on horseback; I admire her spunkiness and courage. The book is in the form of letters that she wrote to her sister back in Edinburgh. She does a masterful job describing the views of the mountains, the sunrises and sunsets, and everything else in between. I was continually struck by how often the grandeur she encounters stops her in her tracks. She has moments, like Isaiah, where she feels undone by the beauty around her. I highly recommend reading this book for the vivid descriptions and to experience the visual pleasures of this part of the country through Bird's eyes.

The next time you travel, think about how you can incorporate enjoying creation into your travel plans. For example, if you are visiting a city, take a walking tour. Pay attention to the beauty of the architecture and the arrangement of the city. I am always interested in the new-to-me types of plants and flowers that grow in various regions. I love to notice the colors and shapes. Worshipping with fellow believers is another way to give shape to your destination and to experience the work of the Church in another context.

If you're looking for a budget-friendly way to travel, try camping. I'll be honest and say when my children were younger it seemed like too much work. I wasn't very good at adjusting my expectations back then. *So what if every meal doesn't have a fruit or a vegetable? So what if it rains? We'll figure it out.* Several years ago, our family went car camping in the Adirondacks. I had the best time and Brad even commented on how relaxed I seemed. The difference this time was I didn't have unrealistic expectations about the experience. I was present in the moment, instead of distracted and worried about the meals we would eat or the weather we would have. I enjoyed my surroundings, talking to God continually in the process. I thanked him for the beautiful creek, the dense woods, the smell of marshmallows roasting, and for fresh coffee in the morning. It also helped that I had some simple meals planned and everyone pitched in to assist with the cooking and clean up.

In his classic devotional *My Utmost for His Highest*, Oswald Chambers writes, "We look for visions from heaven, for earthquakes and thunders of God's power, and never dream that all the time God is in the commonplace things and people around us."[8] Yes! God is in the pink and orange sunrises, the red cardinal sitting on the pine branch, and the single purple bloom of the iris. In the coming days and weeks, may you encounter God's presence as you seek him in creation.

FOR FURTHER REFLECTION

1. Take some time in the coming week to notice the creation outside your window. What do you see? When you step outside, what sounds do you hear? What smells fill your nose? What does that flower petal feel like? Thank God for what you see, hear, smell, feel, and taste. Begin to make this a daily practice.

2. The Psalms are a wonderful place to read about God's splendor and majesty in creation. Psalms 8, 19, and 139, in particular, contain powerful images related to creation. Pray and meditate on the Psalmist's words while you read.

3. Cut out pictures of creation's beauty from magazines, cards, or old calendars. Paste them into a journal, frame them, or put them on your refrigerator to remind you to thank God for his good creation.

4. Create an arrangement for your home that uses elements from creation. Whether it is a flower arrangement or an assortment of rocks, flowers, leaves, and branches, create something lovely for you to enjoy.

5. Spend some time reflecting on the term *earthkeeping*. What would *earthkeeping* look like in your home and community? Are there some first steps you can take to be more mindful of care for creation in your daily habits?

READING SUGGESTIONS

I referenced several books in this chapter that have been helpful to me. While some of them are not solely about creation, they contain sections that cover this topic and are worthy books to read on their own. I am also including some of my favorite travel memoirs since the writers of these books beautifully capture the sights, sounds, and flavors of the places they experience.

CREATION AND THE SPIRITUAL LIFE

Caring for Creation in Your Own Backyard, Loren and Mary Ruth Wilkinson—Organized by the seasons of the year, this book is a "go-to" resource for its theologically rich treatment and understanding of creation and for its practical suggestions. Keep this book in a place where you can access it often. It's that kind of book.

Dakota: A Spiritual Geography, Kathleen Norris—Most people wouldn't put North Dakota on the top of their "must see" state list. But Kathleen Norris has found beauty and spiritual insight in the sometimes harsh landscape of this space. Her writing is reflective and even-keeled, allowing the reader to thoughtfully digest her well-written words.

The Hidden Art of Homemaking, Edith Schaeffer—This book is where it all started for me. Don't be deterred by the parts that sound dated; the truths are timeless. Edith shows in her forthright-yet-engaging, manner that encountering God's presence can happen anywhere. I can hear her saying, "Of course we can witness God's splendor in the single red rose placed in the lovely vase on the table!" Even for a weeknight dinner.

GARDENING/FLOWER ARRANGEMENT

Animal, Vegetable, Miracle, Barbara Kingsolver—I have always enjoyed Kingsolver's fiction, so it wasn't a hard sell for me to read her nonfiction too. This is the story of Barbara, her husband, and her daughter growing, harvesting, and producing almost all of their food for a year on their farm in South Appalachia. The book also includes recipes, which is always a bonus for me.

Bringing Nature Home, Ngoe Minh Ngo—I first heard of this book through Margie Haack's annual "Christmas Gift List" article. The beautiful pictures and variety of vessels used to contain and display the arrangements makes this a lovely coffee table book.

Better Homes and Gardens, (bhg.com)—I have subscribed to BHG for years. From decorating to gardening to food, the magazine and their website are filled with helpful suggestions and ideas.

TRAVEL MEMOIRS

A Lady's Life in the Rocky Mountains, Isabella L. Bird—You may have to hunt a bit for this book, but it's worth it. For starters, the book captures the art of letter writing. As a reader, you will appreciate even more those who knew how to do it well. Such vivid descriptions! Second, if you want to read an adventure story that features a strong woman, this is for you. I only wish to be as brave as Isabella.

A Thousand Days in Tuscany, Marlena de Blasi—Until I have my own Tuscany experience to write about, books like this one will have to suffice. The descriptions, the food, the wine, and the recipes make this place come alive for the reader.

A Year in Provence, Peter Mayle—Peter Mayle has written a number of books, but this one is my favorite. His sense of humor and love of food and drink draw the reader into the beautiful landscape of France. Who wouldn't want to live in Provence?

Under the Tuscan Sun, Frances Mayes—You may have seen the

movie version (Diane Lane portrayed Frances Mayes), but you should really read the book. As a writer and a gourmet cook, Mayes knows how to whet the reader's appetite with beautiful descriptions.

AN ORGANIZATION WORTH CHECKING OUT

A Rocha (arocha.org)—I first heard of A Rocha at Regent College. I even attended a public lecture at the college where the director spoke about the work they do. Here's a brief description from their website:

> A Rocha is a family of Christian conservation organizations begun in 1983 in Portugal where our name means "the rock". Our mission in the US is to inspire, equip and engage Christians and all who will work with us to steward the Earth where they live. We currently work in 20 countries around the globe conducting scientific research, running hands-on conservation projects and operating environmental education programs—all in community settings and with a holistic approach to improve the wellbeing of both people and places.

Encountering God in Literature

> It's not books you need, it's some of the
> things that once were in books....Take it
> where you can find it, in old phonograph
> records, old motion pictures, and in old
> friends; look for it in nature and look for
> it in yourself. Books were only one type
> of receptacle where we stored a lot of
> things we were afraid we might forget.
> The magic is only in what books say, how
> they stitched the patches of the universe
> together into one garment for us.
> —Ray Bradbury, *Fahrenheit 45*[19]

The power of story: what else can cause us to stop every-thing and hold our breath in anticipation of what will happen next? What else can cause a room filled with people to quiet to the point of hearing a pin drop? A good story portrays what is true; what is beautiful; what is good. It points to the author of all: God himself.

As a young reader, the pages of the *Little House on the Prai-*

rie series became my story too. If you peeked into my room or the woods beside my house, you would find me washing the dinner dishes with Mary or pretending to camp somewhere along the prairie. How I wished that Laura's adventures with her family, traveling by wagon to a new home, were my own! Each story in the series whetted my appetite for more. Through reading, I have traveled all over the world and met fascinating characters. I have come face-to-face with my fallen nature and my selfish ways. I have cheered when a character exhibits perseverance, experiences redemption, or expresses love. My life is richer because of reading and I have a difficult time answering the question, "what is your favorite book?" I can't pick *one* book when there are so many good ones that I love! When students complain that they *hate* reading or an acquaintance mentions that she has never been much of reader, I feel a strong compulsion (an obsession perhaps?) to change their view of reading. Suddenly, titles pour out of my mouth as I attempt to convince them that if they read *this one book* their opinion of reading will change forever.

LITERATURE: WHAT IS IT?

Over the years, faithful Christians have been fond of repeating the phrase, "all truth is God's truth."[10] Augustine first coined this phrase, and I love it because it encapsulates so much of what I've learned in my devotional life. Though we wouldn't know the fullness of the Gospel without God's revealed word in the Scriptures, God's truth isn't limited to Sunday worship services and the Bible. God's truth also comes to us through conversations, through music, through movies, through creation, and yes, through literature.

Literature is well-crafted story. However, not all books are created equal. Navigating the world of reading requires discernment and wisdom. At times, this means putting a book aside or choosing not to read certain subjects or authors. Let me be clear: some books have very little truth in them. If evil, untruth, or lies dominate, don't waste your time reading those books. On the other hand, just because a particular book contains elements of evil or has characters that are morally bankrupt should not alone be reason to avoid it. The Bible, for example, contains some truly awful deeds (e.g., child sacrifices, incest, murder), and God's own chosen people disobey his commands repeatedly, resulting in painful consequences. Yet God's truth and redemption reign throughout Scripture and there is no doubt what God thinks about sin and evil.

When we read, there needs to be helpful checks and balances. As a married woman, it would be unwise for me only to read books that portray married women having affairs and leaving their families. Why fill my mind with images of marital discontent and illicit moments with another lover? Conversely, just because a book contains a married woman committing adultery shouldn't be the only reason I choose to not read that particular book. As tempted as we may be to say, "I will only read 'Christian' books," I think there is another way to approach what we read. There are guidelines we can use to help us make wise choices as readers.

Let's go back to my adultery example. One question to ask is, "How honestly is adultery portrayed in the book?" Is adultery depicted as acceptable and even preferable to marital faithfulness? Does this book show the devastating consequences adultery has on a person and a family? If a book fails to address a particular subject matter honestly, that should signal it's time to find another book. Another issue to pay attention to is the graphic nature of a novel, particularly erotica. Reading page upon page of romantically explicit scenes, especially between an unmarried couple, is a red flag. Paul exhorts us in Philippians 4:8 to think about whatever is true, whatever is honorable, whatever is just, whatever is pure. If the overwhelming content of a book goes against what is true, what is right, and what is pure, we need to pay heed. After all, our minds will be filled with the images we read. This doesn't mean I don't read books containing some graphic subject matter. Certain non-fiction, such as biographies or historical pieces, can be violent and disturbing. Books describing scenes from the concentration camps during WWII are difficult to read! Yet the Holocaust is true. Horrible acts committed against innocent people took place. Let me also affirm you need to listen to your heart and mind as it relates to the content of a book. Monitor your inner voice as you read. Do you find yourself tempted? Lust isn't the only kind of temptation. Feelings of envy, greed, anger, and anxiety can cause us to sin. Scripture speaks of the devil as a prowling lion, seeking someone to devour (1 Pet. 5:8). Don't think the devil's schemes are off limits when we read! What is emotionally, even spiritually healthy for one person to read, may not be healthy for another person to read. I don't read books that portray or describe child abuse in detail. Since becoming a mother, I have a heightened sensitivity to this issue. I understand myself well enough to know that those images will stay with me for a long time. So I choose to read something else.

Lastly, our conscience can serve as a powerful indicator of whether or not we should read a particular book. We should not underestimate the power of the Holy Spirit in our lives. He will convict and guide us in our reading choices. Pay attention to the nudging or the niggling sense that something isn't right. The Holy Spirit is speaking to you and you should listen. Reading literature is not a time to turn off the brain no matter how tempting it may be to reach for the serial romance novel. We need to engage our minds and hearts while we read.

LITERATURE: WHY IS IT IMPORTANT?

I can still recall the surprise I felt when a close friend told me she didn't read fiction because it wasn't true. Perhaps you feel the same way or you are suspect of the imagination. If this is the case, remember that God is the creator of imagination and we, as humans, are made in his image. God's truth isn't limited to facts and statistics. He made us creatures who love stories. Gladys Hunt, the author of *Honey for a Child's Heart*, also wrote *Honey for a Woman's Heart*. I highly recommend both of these books for their wisdom about reading and for their book recommendations. In *Honey for a Woman's Heart*, Hunt says, "I read it [fiction] because it helps me pay attention to life. Reading good fiction is not simply a frivolous activity for those who aren't serious about life. I read because I am serious, and find that fiction says true things I might never hear any other way."[11] A story invites us to have, through our imaginations, a concrete experience of truth.

THE POWER OF WORDS

The power of words and what they communicate to us makes literature important. In the first chapter of this book, we looked at the creation story and acknowledged God as creator of the universe. Along with all the plants, flowers, and trees, God also created words. In John 1:1 we read, "In the beginning was the Word, and the Word was with God and the Word was God." God made us to use words and to respond to them. We learn about the person, Jesus Christ through the Word. While he was on earth, Jesus preached and interacted with people. In literature, words introduce and reveal the characters in the story to us. We learn about the characters through the descriptions given by the author, by the narrator, by the character himself, and from the words of the other characters.

As Hunt says, words give meaning to our lives. They have the power to impact us both positively and negatively. We can all share stories about instances when we wish we could grab our words and stuff them safely back into our mouths or times when someone's words were just what we needed to hear at that moment. In James' letter to the church, he writes about the power of the tongue. He compares the tongue to a bit in a horse's mouth or a rudder that steers a ship. Each of these items is small in comparison to the animal or object it controls. Yet each holds great power. In addition, the book of Proverbs is filled with sayings about words and their implications. "The words of a gossip are like choice morsels; they go down to the inmost parts" (Prov. 18:8 NIV). "Gracious words are like a honeycomb, sweetness to the soul and health to the body" (Prov. 16:24). "Those who have knowledge use words with restraint, and those who have understanding are even-tempered" (Prov. 17:27 NIV). Our words matter.

Literature also mirrors the great Biblical narrative, which is told largely as story. Start with Genesis and finish with Revelation and you will see the variety of ways God's redemptive plan is told to his people throughout the Bible. From lyric poetry to storytelling to letters, the Bible employs a variety of genres to communicate God's word. When we read the Gospels, we see Jesus using story to explain truth to people. In the beginning verses of chapter four of Mark's Gospel, we read, "Again Jesus began to teach by the sea . . . He was teaching them many things in parables." The chapter ends with Jesus explaining the kingdom of God to his listeners in parable form: "With what can we compare the kingdom of God... it is like a grain of mustard seed. . ." (Mark 4:30–31).

LITERATURE: WAYS WE CAN ENCOUNTER GOD

Good literature opens the door for us to encounter God and it starts by reading. As we immerse ourselves in quality literature, we become more adept at recognizing God and his truth in stories and characters. I love the story of Nathan and David in 2 Samuel 12 because it is such a clear example of how literature helps us to see ourselves—both the good and the bad. David has taken Bathsheba as his wife and had Uriah, Bathsheba's husband, killed. The Lord sends Nathan, the prophet, to David to confront him. Notice how Nathan does this. He begins, "There were two men in a certain city, the one rich and the other poor. The rich man had very many flocks and herds" (vv. 1–2). Nathan doesn't even tell David, "Now I want to tell you a story." He just begins and the story continues until we learn that the rich man takes the poor man's lamb to feed a traveler. The text tells us that when David heard this, "He burned with anger against the man and said to Nathan, 'As surely as the Lord lives, the man who did this must die! He must pay for that lamb four times over, because he did such a thing and had no pity.' Then Nathan said to David, "You are the man" (vv. 2–7 NIV)!

Wow! Could you ask for a better mirror? Through story, a door opens, allowing us to accept truth and harsh words that we would not otherwise hear if a friend or family member confronted us. David hears and is struck to the heart. He confesses his sin and repents. God can use literature to convict us about patterns of sin in our own lives, and like David, we have the opportunity to repent and start afresh.

GOOD VS. EVIL

When we read literature, good and evil are revealed, and thus the God who rules over all is also revealed to us. We become mindful of God's goodness to us and to his world, and we look forward to the day when all suffering and evil will end and all shall be made right.

When I was teaching sixth grade, I read aloud the story *A Single Shard* by Linda Sue Park.[12] I was particularly struck one day as I was reading when the main character, who is on a journey to deliver an important piece of pottery, runs into some nasty characters who throw his carefully packed pieces over a cliff. As I read the scene to my students, one student audibly exclaimed, "Oh!" The room was completely quiet and I had everyone's attention. I did not need to stop and say, "Now students, that was a bad character and what he did was wrong." They knew! They themselves recognized the evil. Tolkien is a master at this. If you have read *The Lord of the Rings* trilogy, you know what I mean. Frodo and Sam are brave and courageous and willing to risk their lives for the greater good. Sauron, on the other hand, is consumed by the greed of the ring and will not stop until he owns it. As we read, we celebrate goodness and truth, all of which point us to God. Our emotions are stirred and we find ourselves mulling over what we have read.

WITNESS REDEMPTION

We encounter God through literature by witnessing redemption. These reminders of divine mercy help us examine our own lives. A book that shows the redemption of a character is *The Shipping News* by Annie Proulx. She won the Pulitzer Prize for this novel in 1994, and it was also made into a movie. This isn't an easy book to read, however. It is graphic in its descriptions and truly terrible things happen to some of the characters. In the novel, we meet Quolye, a pathetic character in many respects, and slowly watch his life transform into something good.

> Hive-spangled, gut roaring with gas and cramp, he survived childhood; at the state university, hand clapped over his chin, he camouflaged torment with smiles and silence. Stumbled through his twenties and into his thirties learning to separate his feelings from his life, counting on nothing.[13]

As a reader, initially we feel disgust towards Quolye. He is a doormat, allowing others to abuse and walk all over him. Yet by the end of the novel he has been transformed. He stands up for himself and no longer habitually claps his hand over his chin.

> Quolye experienced moments in all colors, uttered brilliancies, paid attention to the rich sound of waves counting stones, he laughed and wept, noticed sunsets, heard music in rain, said I do.[14]

In reading the redemption stories of others, we are reminded of our own need for redemption. There is nothing we can do to make ourselves right in God's eyes. We are finite beings and in need of a Savior. We can also thank God for his ongoing redemptive work in our lives.

A BIGGER WORLD

As a woman in her forties, I am still waiting for my dream trip to Europe. However, do you know how many times I have traveled abroad in books? As I read the stories of others, I experience their travels and adventures vicariously. Earlier in the chapter I mentioned historical fiction and how it can inform us about historical people and events. As we read these stories, in addition to the true stories of others, we can be prompted to act in our world. Pain and suffering exist in all corners. Who knows how God may move you to act as a result of reading about a situation or a group of people who are suffering. It may not even be people on the other side of the world; it may be our neighbors and coworkers. As we read, we may experience God's Spirit stirring us. Pay attention to those stirrings. Use those moments to pray for the people or situation. Ask God to keep the need fresh in your mind and listen for his further promptings.

Encountering God in literature can be the kind of experience that penetrates deeply and leaves you thoughtful for days. Some stories are written in such a way that they seep into your bones and quicken your soul; you feel in a haze as your mind and heart process what you have read. But you may be in a season of life that makes reading hard, even when you desire to be totally engaged by a book. Let me offer some suggestions if reading seems akin to climbing Mt. Everest.

EXPERIMENT WITH TECHNOLOGY

After my first child was born, I felt like I entered a "non-reading phase." If I read at night, I fell asleep. If I read during the day, I felt guilty because surely a toilet needed cleaning or laundry needed folding. It made a huge difference when I wasn't getting up in the middle of the night for feedings and wasn't so tired. It also made a difference when I moved beyond feeling guilty for choosing to read instead of completing a household task. Reading is a worthwhile activity in its own right. Granted, my family still needed to eat and someone still needed to do the laundry, but taking some time out in the afternoon to read was feeding my mind and my spirit—two very important components in the life of a young stay-at-home-mom.

I wish I had tried listening to an audiobook during that season. Try downloading a book to your device of choice and listen while exercising or cleaning the house or driving in the car. Long car trips can become more bearable when a good story is being told. Many digital books are read by the authors or by actors who make the story come alive with their dramatic expressions and voice inflection. Also, if Bible reading is a struggle, like it was for me during those years of early morning wake-up calls, there are all sorts of Bible apps available, including ones that will read the text aloud.

SEEK OUT BOOK RECOMMENDATIONS

If it's challenging to find a good book to read, technology can help! Today, websites such as Goodreads make finding book recommendations so much easier. The site provides you with a brief description of the book and can show you what your friends are reading and why they liked or did not like a book. You can also ask others who know you for book recommendations. Whenever I talk about books with others, I generally share my "fifty page rule." (I didn't come up with this guideline, someone else did.) If a book doesn't grab my attention in the first fifty pages, I drop it and move on. I've been known to extend that to one hundred pages, depending on the book. In my opinion, there are too many good books to read and not enough time, so don't sweat it over something you don't like. The first time I did this I felt a twinge of guilt (I was an English major in college who was trained always to finish a book), but now I just move on to the next book. I have a memo page in my phone where I record book titles, making it easy to access anywhere. You never know where you will hear about a good book.

Once, while traveling on an airplane, my seatmate recommended a book to me when she saw me engrossed in the novel I was reading. I added the title to my running list. National Public Radio frequently reviews new books and interviews their authors, providing a source for recommendations and giving listeners a chance to learn the background for the book. I regularly ask other reading friends or people I respect, "What are you reading?" While this may strike you as somewhat obvious, my life is richer because of asking this simple question. Books I never would have found on my own have become favorites.

DISCOVER CHILDREN'S LITERATURE

Children's literature is a great place to start if finding a book you like seems overwhelming. Authors like C.S. Lewis and Madeline L'Engle have a way of presenting truth so that it resonates with children and adults alike. A couple of years ago, while preparing a chapel talk on heaven, I reread the ending of *The Last Battle*. Aslan's explanation of "further up and further in" and the final lines of the book—"Now at last they were beginning Chapter One of the Great Story, which no one on earth has read: which goes on forever: in which every chapter is better than the one before"[15]—filled me with a longing for heaven that I had not experienced up to that point. This leads me to an oft-used analogy I share with my students: books are like onions. Each time you reread a book you peel off another layer of the onion and discover something you missed previously. This time, as I read *The Last Battle*, I felt as if God were whispering to me, "Yes, heaven is *that* good."

JOIN A BOOK CLUB

Joining a book club is a wonderful motivator for reading. Most groups meet monthly and it really helps to have a deadline to finish a book. I have been known to finish one in the hours leading up to book club! If you don't know of any books clubs in your area, don't be afraid to start one. I started my first book club in Elgin, Illinois. One day, as I was chatting with a neighbor, I got up my nerve and asked if she would like to be part of a book club. Immediately she responded with a "Yes!" and she knew some other neighbors who would also want to join. For our first meeting, I intentionally outlined some parameters for choosing books. I relied heavily on Gladys Hunt's wisdom from *Honey for a Woman's Heart* as well. I wanted to make sure we read quality literature and I sought to define what that was. We opted to put forth book recommendations and then vote on the titles and descriptions that appealed to us, forming our reading list for the year. Once we were more established, we did this in December and marked the occasion with fondue. While dipping fruit or pound cake into chocolate, we cast our votes for the coming year's books. A fine tradition!

To my knowledge, there were only a couple of us who were believers in the group. I warned my Christian friends who wanted to join us, "Do not try to use this book club as a chance to evangelize! That is not our purpose." As often is the case when discussing good literature, spiritual matters came up in the course of our discussions. I earnestly prayed for discernment and a winsome spirit in those moments. I also realized I had some personal homework to do in regards to apologetics. During one discussion, a woman asked, "Is Jesus really the only way to eternal life?" How to answer this question without sounding arrogant and self-righteous! While my friends and I may not have handled every question or comment perfectly, the fact that the group, plus or minus some members over the years, still meets some fifteen years later, speaks for itself.

Finally, don't feel bad if everyone complains about not liking the book in a given month. What is it about the book they didn't like? I have found *those* books to stimulate the best discussions. And, not surprisingly, have seen opinions change after the discussion and, in the end, one person even admitted, "the book wasn't *that* bad."

I can still recall the sadness I felt as I turned the final pages of *The First Four Years*—the last book in the *Little House on the Prairie* series. My adventures with Laura drew to a close. From pretending to be her in my imaginary play to watching her become a grown woman, married with a child, I felt as if I knew her. That's the power of story. I would return to those books several times throughout my childhood, and again as an adult with my own children, reliving the joys and hardships of the Ingalls' family.

What are you waiting for? A whole world of books waits to be read! Curl up in your favorite spot with a cup of coffee or tea and lose yourself in story. May you encounter the author of story—God himself—as you meet new people and discover new places.

FOR FURTHER REFLECTION

1. Think about the last book you read. What truths about God's character and/or human nature were revealed through the characters or actions of the characters in the novel?

2. Start a commonplace book. Essentially, a commonplace book is a scrapbook. Record favorite quotes, passages, and words from the books you read. You can even organize your commonplace book around themes or topics. For more information on creating a commonplace book, search the internet for "keeping a Commonplace Book" for a variety ideas and suggestions on this topic.

3. If reading is a challenge for you, what is one step you could take to incorporate reading into your everyday life?

4. Want to dig a little deeper? One way to become a better reader is to recognize the attributes of quality literature in the books you read. Good literature will contain most, if not all, of these attributes. (I learned of these terms from Spalding Education International and their curriculum,

The Writing Road to Reading. As an educator, I loved Spalding's approach to teaching about quality literature.)[16] Here's a quick overview: *Precise language*: Language that is concrete, specific, and vivid. *Emotional Appeal*: Language and situations evoke emotions from the reader (happiness, sadness, compassion). *Embedded Information*: Information (such as science, geography, history) is embedded in the literature. *Insight into Life and People*: Dialogue and situations enable the reader to determine motives, desires, and rewards and consequences for different behaviors. *Universality*: Common traits or experiences are understood and recognized by readers across time and cultures—think of the classics. As you read your next novel, look for examples of these attributes.

READING RESOURCES

The following books are wonderful resource and reference books. You can flip through these repeatedly to find book suggestions or to inspire and motivate you to become a better reader. Some of the books are especially helpful if you have children in the home and want to instill a love of reading at an early age. On the other hand, it is never too late to become a reader!

Honey for a Child's Heart, Gladys Hunt

Honey for a Teen's Heart, Gladys Hunt and Barbara Hampton

Honey for a Woman's Heart, Gladys Hunt

Walking on Water: Reflections on Faith and Art, Madeleine L'Engle—If you want to read more about the intersection of faith and the arts, this book is a good place to start.

A Time to Read: Good Books for Growing Readers, Mary Ruth Wilkinson & Heidi Wilkinson Teel

Books Children Love, Elizabeth Wilson

FAVORITE READ-ALOUDS

I would be remiss to end this chapter without sharing some of my favorite read-alouds that my family or my students have enjoyed over the years. Some of these books are better suited for older children, so you may want to do some online investigating before you begin reading aloud. In no particular order, here are my "Top 10 Read-Alouds."

The Chronicles of Narnia, C.S. Lewis
The Lord of the Rings trilogy, JRR Tolkien
Understood Betsy, Dorothy Canfield Fisher
The Great Brain, John D. Fitzgerald
The *Little House on the Prairie* series, Laura Ingalls Wilder
The *Harry Potter* series, J.K. Rowling
A Wrinkle in Time, Madeleine L'Engle
Wednesday Wars, Gary Schmidt
Twenty and Ten, Claire Hutchet Bishop
Roll of Thunder, Hear my Cry, Mildred D. Taylor

Encountering God in Hospitality

> CALPURNIA: There's some folks who don't
> eat like us, but you ain't called on to con-
> tradict 'em at the table when they don't...
> SCOUT: He ain't company, Cal, he's just a
> Cunningham--
> CALPURNIA: Hush your mouth! Don't
> matter who they are, anybody sets foot in
> this house's yo' comp'ny.
> —Harper Lee, *To Kill A Mockingbird*[17]

The lasagna baked in the oven, filling the house with delicious smells. Barely-used wedding dishes graced each place
setting at the dining room table. Butterflies flitted through my
stomach as I reviewed the menu. Had I forgotten anything?
This wasn't the first time I prepared a meal for guests, but this
time it was different. This was the first time the guests were
invited for dinner at my house after recently being married.
Sure, I had helped my parents entertain on countless occasions. I knew my way around the kitchen and understood the
basics of cooking. But this time Mom wasn't hanging out in

the kitchen in case something went wrong.

Well, I didn't burn the dinner or leave out a key ingredient, but I did produce the driest lasagna I ever served. The recipe said to bake the dish for an hour. I did. Unfortunately, I was still too inexperienced as a cook to know that oven temperatures vary or that the size of your pan affects the cooking time. The lasagna was edible, but I'm sure our friends didn't go home raving about my cooking or secretly hoping that I would share the recipe. Truth be told, this wouldn't be the last time I would serve a less than perfect dish or have a fiasco to finesse before company arrived.

The fact that I still remember this incident twenty-five years later tells you a bit about me. I have a hard time letting go of my mistakes. But here's the truth about this situation. I highly doubt that our dinner guests even remember the dry lasagna. Instead, I hope they recall the excited, nervous newlyweds, who were eager to host some friends for dinner in their apartment. Gathered around the table, we laughed and talked and deepened our relationship. The goodness of hospitality manifested itself that night despite a less than ideal main course.

Even today, I still have my share of hospitality failures. But the failures have been powerful teachers. I have learned that offering my guests a fully-present self, instead of a distracted one, is a true gift. As a first-born, I can quickly zero in on the one aspect of the meal that isn't right. Yet now I know that instead of spending the rest of the evening apologizing profusely for a burnt lasagna, my guests and I can laugh together about any mistakes and eat more of the other dishes. The point of hospitality isn't to impress, anyway.

HOSPITALITY: WHAT IS IT?

Not long ago I forgot that I agreed to host a student who needed a place a stay for the night before a school break. She's a junior in high school, but as I quickly snatched up pieces of clothing and bits of dog hair off the floor, you might have thought she was a city health inspector. When you hear the word "guest" or "hospitality" or the phrase "coming for a visit" what images flit through your mind? Maybe it's that pile of dirty laundry on your living room floor or that kitchen sink overflowing with the week's dishes—your heart rate increases and your palms sweat at the very thought of a guest dropping by right *now*! Or perhaps, you imagine fashionably-dressed people mingling in your living room, nibbling on delicious appetizers and sipping fine wine. In your daydreams your house is delightfully decorated and completely current and your guests comment on your impeccable taste. You wonder, "What would it be like to host *that* kind of a dinner party?" Most of us tend to fall into two camps regarding hospitality. Some of us dread it, feeling we can never host quite "good enough;" others of us set impossibly high standards that hold us back from truly enjoying our guests. It seems unavoidable to stop filling our minds with unhelpful images of what we *think* hospitality is and what it should look like. Too often we link hospitality with perfection, resulting in a skewed under-standing of the word and its meaning. Knowing what hospi-tality is removes that burdensome weight of perfection. Prac-ticing *real* hospitality serves as a pathway for experiencing God's presence.

HOSPITALITY WELCOMES

First and foremost, hospitality welcomes. This welcome is the friendly smile on your face when a friend shows up in need, despite the fact your family room is a landmine of LEGO™ pieces and My Little Ponies™. This welcome is the fresh flowers, piece of artisanal chocolate, or scented candle you placed on the bedside table for the delight of your overnight guests. This welcome is paying attention to what your guests like. My friend, Dar, knows how much I love strong coffee in the morning. Whenever I visit, she has a bag of dark roast coffee especially for me in the cupboard. This gesture communicates her love and care. The welcome of hospitality also provides food that says, "I am glad you're seated at my table. I'm making some of my favorite dishes for you." Your "favorites" can be as straightforward as tomato soup and toasted cheese sandwiches or as extravagant as vichyssoise and beef tenderloin. The welcome of hospitality also includes those special occasions like a birthday party or holiday dinner upon which you lavish more of your time, effort, and finances. The welcome of hospitality is both kind and robust—we welcome those we know as well as those we don't know. Hospitality teaches us to welcome those who are charming and those who are a little prickly. Hospitality asks us to welcome those who can return the blessing and those who cannot. When we offer hospitality, we imitate our Lord, who brings us into his own home, even though we are unfit guests for so lordly a manor. He makes us fit.

HOSPITALITY COSTS SOMETHING

There's no way around it, hospitality has a price tag. There is no free lunch! This can be hard to swallow. When we moved to Stony Brook, New York, to work at a boarding school, we learned that one of the requirements of living in a faculty home is to host an annual student Open House. Students come and go, eat, watch a movie, or play a game. I experience mixed emotions every time we host an Open House. A part of me loves hosting students in our home... but another part dreads the evening. With sometimes close to 50 students milling about, food crumbs trail across surfaces or fall in-between sofa cushions, spilled drinks make for sticky floors, and furniture pushed against the walls leave scuff marks or paint dings. I am on my feet, constantly refilling food bowls or emptying overflowing trash cans. By the end of the evening, I am exhausted. Yet without fail, after each Open House a handful of students will tell me how much they appreciate being in our home or thank me for the food, their gratitude making my personal inconveniences look minor in comparison. Yes, hospitality costs my time, my money, my belongings, and my energy. But this cost is minimal when I consider that each student who walks through my door is made in the image of God.

HOSPITALITY IN THE BIBLICAL NARRATIVE

Scripture speaks clearly about hospitality. While the word "hospitality" itself doesn't appear in the Old Testament, several passages distinctly define the concept. In Genesis 18, Abraham entertains three strangers. If you think hospitality is *only* for women, think again. Abraham is the central figure here. And bear in mind Comfort Inn and Suites or Holiday Inn Express did not exist in ancient times. Travel was dangerous; it wasn't safe to camp beside the road, you were dependant on someone else, most likely a stranger, to provide you with both lodging and food. In this story, travelers—three men—show up at Abraham's tent flap. Abraham hurries to meet these strangers, telling them he will bring them water to wash their feet and food to refresh them. During this process of hosting them, he learns that his wife, Sarah, will have a baby and about the upcoming destruction of Sodom and Gomorrah. Quite some news to receive from guests you have never met before! The significance of this passage becomes more evident when you read Hebrews 13:2 (NIV), which references this Old Testament story: "Do not forget to show hospitality to strangers, for by so doing some people have shown hospitality to angels without knowing it." One of Abraham's strangers turns out to be the Lord himself! We often don't know the results of inviting someone to "rest under our tree" but Scripture certainly indicates that "someone" could very well be a celestial ambassador!

My parents had an "angel" encounter when they returned from a trip to Chicago with a group of Taylor University students one winter. I can still recall my incredulity when I heard my mom explain, "We're spending the night at a woman's house—we met her at the gas station. We'll call you in the morning." A snowstorm struck, making travel dangerous. Eventually the Highway Patrol closed the Interstate, forcing travelers off the road. Stopping at a gas station to figure out a plan, a woman overheard their situation and invited them to spend the night at her house. She was a single mom with a teenage daughter. The next morning she fed them breakfast before sending them on their way. *She* was *their* angel, ready to meet their needs at just the right moment.

Another facet of hospitality in the Old Testament is apparent when Moses gives the Israelites the commandants and laws of the Lord. In Deuteronomy 10:18–19 we read, "[God] defends the cause of the fatherless and the widow, and loves the foreigners residing among you, giving them food and clothing. And you are to love those who are foreigners, for you yourselves were foreigners in Egypt" (NIV). Notice the command here. God is telling his people to practice hospitality as *he* practiced hospitality with them when he led them out of Egypt. The Israelites lived for 400 years as slaves in Egypt. Not in their homeland and certainly not on their terms. Yet God graciously provided for them, and gave them a leader, Moses, who led them out of their bondage and eventually into the Promised Land.

"Foreigners" are in our midst today. Wherever you live, there are people new to the neighborhood, trying to figure out where to shop, which doctor to go to, or what church to attend. Perhaps *you* are the "foreigner." Moving is a significant part of my own story. Each move to date has generated a mixture of excitement and uncertainty. Each time, I have been the recipient of generous help and advice, meeting that one person who recommended the best places to shop or knew information critical to settling my family into our new home. As I write these words, the refugee crisis in Syria fills my mind. Thousands of families and individuals have been forced out of their homes by ISIS. Pictures of young children pulled from boats and elderly individuals stumbling along rocky beaches break our hearts. Many European countries struggle to assimilate and assist the thousands now on their doorsteps. On the one hand, we are shocked and angered by the actions of ISIS. On the other hand, the reality of finding jobs, decent housing, and medical care for these refugees is a logistical challenge. Thousands of miles away in New York I struggle with the best way to respond. Giving money to organizations working to provide aid feels too easy and doesn't involve much "mess" on my part. But what if my neighborhood was suddenly filled with individuals needing places to stay? Individuals who don't speak the same language as me or who have different customs from my own? How would I feel about my new neighbors? These are tough questions, demanding thoughtful and prayerful responses. I'm grateful for the churches and organizations that have opened their doors, not backing away from the complexities of this situation.

Throughout the New Testament, we read stories and instructions about hospitality. In Romans 12:13, Paul encourages the believers to *practice* it. He gives this exhortation right in the middle of other reminders about Christian living. He directs, "Share with the Lord's people who are in need. Practice hospitality" (NIV). This verse indicates a general pattern taught throughout the New Testament: Give to all and especially to fellow believers. In 1 Peter 4:9, the standard set is to, "Show hospitality to one another without grumbling." Peter understands that hospitality can be draining, and some people are ungrateful or even take advantage of your open heart. Yet that doesn't relieve us of our responsibility to reach out to others.

One of the most famous New Testament characters known for hospitality is Martha, Jesus's friend. Jesus regularly dined at her home in Bethany. Some have unjustly maligned Martha in light of the incident recorded in Luke 10:38–42, where she is overwhelmed by all the preparations and is mad at her sister. Instead of helping Martha, Mary sits at Jesus' feet, listening and learning. When Martha complains to Jesus about the unfairness of the workload, Jesus tells her that her priorities are wrong; that there are better things to be done than scurrying around trying to pull off a meal.

Martha is like many of us. She veers off track momentarily

and forgets the purpose of hospitality. She needs a reminder of what is truly important. It's not about the preparations, it's not about the food, it's about Jesus and being with him. We see another side of Martha in John 11 and 12. Lazarus, her brother, has just died. Martha hears that Jesus is coming to Bethany and she goes out to meet him. The text says, "but Mary remained seated in the house" (John 11:20). Not only does Martha go out to meet Jesus, but she also declares that Jesus is the Messiah. Those of us who are prone to the "doing" side of the spectrum can take comfort. In this moment, Martha's active side is to be praised. She goes back to the house and tells her sister, "Come on, let's go see Jesus." Later, in chapter 12, Jesus was once again in Bethany and a dinner was given in his honor. The text simply says, "Martha served." This time, I think she got it right.

I still have vivid recollections of my Martha moment. Our family was living in Vancouver and Christmas was fast approaching. In a few moments, our family needed to hop in the car and drive to Seattle to pick up my parents and brother from the airport. The holidays are always a busy time of year and this year was no different. I was homeschooling two children, working part time, and running a household. Mere minutes before we piled into the car, I was literally running throughout the house, dusting, changing sheets, picking up odds and ends, you name it. Collapsing into the front seat of the car, I was sweaty and out of breath. Why did I make myself into a crazy woman? These were my parents and brother visiting, who love me regardless of whether or not the toilet bowl is clean! To be honest, I valued having my house looking "perfect" rather than acknowledging that I couldn't do everything. I began that visit distracted and upset, like Martha, instead of relaxed and excited about spending time with my family.

HOSPITALITY: WHY IS IT IMPORTANT?

We all know people who exude hospitality. They are the friends or acquaintances who ask you an insightful question and then really listen to your answer; who make you feel special, like you are the only person in the room who matters to them; who fixes you a delicious lunch without you even noticing that they're doing it. We console ourselves by saying, "Well, that's her personality, her gift, of course hospitality comes easily for *her*." Before we let ourselves off the hook, practicing hospitality isn't just for extroverts, skilled cooks, or for those for whom it "comes naturally." Hospitality is *important*. As believers, God's presence is with us. We don't "practice" hospitality alone. God promises to never give us more than we can bear. We must trust that he will supply us with the strength and grace we need, even when we feel our lack.

Tim Keller, the pastor at Redeemer Presbyterian in New York City, preached a series on Christian practices, including hospitality. Keller noted that hospitality is important because it builds community.[18] Whether it is building community in a small group or a Sunday school class, or with your neighbors or friends, we need a place where we can be ourselves. For the first twenty years of our marriage, Brad and I were a part of either a Sunday school class or a small group. In some of those groups the community bonds ran deep, but we also had our share of groups that were less than ideal, that required an extra effort to show up to week in and week out. Still, we knew we weren't wired to be lone rangers. Being a part of a group mattered. Showing up each week to group mattered. Practicing hospitality with those who required extra love and grace on our part grew us in ways that could not have happened otherwise.

FOOD AND HOSPITALITY: A SACRED LINK

Food and hospitality are intrinsically linked. When we come together as guest and host to share a meal, this exchange gains a sacramental quality. Something powerful and mysterious happens when we gather around a table. We experience what theologians call "common grace" as we eat, talk, and listen to one another. This sacred space becomes a pathway into *more*. In the intimacy of comfort—not just physical comfort but also emotional and spiritual comfort—someone announces that her mother has been diagnosed with cancer; someone confides he is struggling with depression; another shares the good news of a new job.

I'm always amazed when I host a dinner and once again, we all end up sitting around the dining room table for the entire evening and never even venture into the living room. No one wants to move. In the hustle and bustle of our full lives, we savor the lingering and talking without the pressure to move on to the next thing. This is encouraging for those of us who mistakenly believe our entire house needs to be cleaned before we invite guests for dinner. The reality is your guests will probably only be in one or two rooms once they cross your threshold: wherever the meal is set and the bathroom.

And please, again, it bears repeating, we do not have to serve a gourmet meal in order to practice hospitality. Consider the elements we eat and drink at the Lord's Supper—bread and wine—common, everyday food items. I fondly remember when our family was invited to lunch after church by some friends and our hostess apologizing for the menu—"it's just grilled cheese and tomato soup, but we would love to have you over." We had *the best* time together. The kids happily played and the adults enjoyed lively conversation. It didn't matter in the least that we weren't eating roast beef for lunch. We were glad to be together. The proverbial soup and sandwich menu played second fiddle to the warmth of the welcome. What a blessing.

HOSPITALITY: WAYS TO ENCOUNTER GOD

John Piper describes hospitality like this: "it is asking out and asking in."[19] When we do this, ask out and ask in, we catch glimpses of God's presence and work in our own lives and in the lives of our guests. We begin by asking people into our space—often, but not always, that means our home. If a dinner seems too much, ask people over for dessert or for morning coffee. Potlucks are a great way to share the responsibilities of a meal. During our years of graduate-school living, potlucks were the only way possible for us budget-conscious students to gather socially. The burden of providing all of the food was lifted. Even now, whenever I ask someone for dinner, invariably he or she asks, "what can I bring?" Conversely, if you are the one providing the space, feel free to ask someone else to bring the dessert or the snack. Each small group I have been part of rotated who brought the treats. If you hosted, then someone else brought goodies. And those who lent a hand cleaning up without being asked were always well appreciated.

Hospitality doesn't always have to be an invitation into our home. It can be inviting others into a space *with* you—out for coffee or a picnic with take-out food. Listen to them. Ask questions. You can also practice hospitality creatively in the workplace and thereby bless your colleagues. Eat your lunch in the staff cafeteria with someone new. Invite someone out to lunch. Keep your eyes open for the new person and make a point of getting to know them over a coffee or workday meal. If you always eat with the same people, expand that group. These simple, thoughtful gestures testify to God's love and care for others.

In your neighborhood, thinking seasonally can spur you to practice hospitality, and I don't mean just Christmas. The first two years Brad and I were married, we lived in the downstairs floor of a mint-green house in Van Wert, Ohio. Brad was a youth pastor and I was finishing my degree before taking a job as a teacher. Finances were tight. Brad got the idea to invite our neighbors over to watch one of the final games of the World Series. I was nervous—would anyone come? Besides, we didn't really *know* our neighbors. Guess what? They came! I can't even remember what I served, probably some chips and soda. It didn't matter. What *did* matter was that our neighbors came and watched the game with us.

Once we moved to Illinois and purchased our first home, we hosted a neighborhood Christmas Open House. Each year I worried if anyone would show up. The first hour was hard because almost no one came by, but eventually the pace picked up, people arrived and they always stayed past the time specified on the invitation. Over and over again, people would say, "Thank you for doing this. We need to do this more often." Looking back, I can't tell you if any "spiritual fruit" grew from our Open Houses. That wasn't the point. We wanted to know our neighbors and to be known by our neighbors. We created a welcoming space to initiate and nurture that mutual knowing. God *was* present, though, and whether or not anyone else realized this, my own faith was strengthened simply by offering a neighbor a kind word and some Christmas cheer. Don't be afraid—be bold and think creatively about "reasons" to extend an invitation to others to be guests in your home. If it sounds alarming to add "open house" to *your* Christmas schedule, the four seasons and the twelve months of the year provide plenty of opportunities— what about an Easter open house, a summer barbeque, or a fall potluck? What about going really big and throwing a neighborhood block party!

If you are married, include single people in your practice of hospitality. Holidays can be especially lonely. When we lived in Waco, we knew a number of Baylor University and Truett Seminary students. One Christmas we stayed home instead of traveling to extended family, and we invited two Chinese graduate students to join us for Christmas dinner. Their gratefulness was evident. When I ask my single friends if they mind hanging out with my family, the resounding answer is no, they love being included with families. Keep this in mind the next time you host an event; think about the single people you know who would enjoy spending time in your home.

Within the church, we have opportunities to practice hospitality as the body of Christ. For a while we attended a church in Waco that was situated in the poorest neighborhood in the community. The first Sunday of every month a simple meal was served after church. It was called "First Sunday Lunch." For those visiting the church for the first, second, or third time, this meal provided an opportunity to get to know fellow church members. For others, this meal met a real need—a nourishing, filling lunch.

Consider being a greeter or helping out in the Welcome Center if your church has one. New people especially need to see a friendly face when they enter church. No matter who you are, walking through the doors of a new church for the first time is an intimidating experience. Will anyone notice me? What do I say? What about my children? Will they be okay in the nursery or Sunday School? I have attended many churches over the years; yet, I will never forget the warm welcome my family received the first Sunday we visited a church in Texas. Sharyn greeted us with characteristic southern warmth. She helped us take our children to Sunday School and she delivered Brad and me to Newcomers, a Sunday School class specifically designed for new people. We met other first-timers like ourselves and learned about ways we could plug into the church. We heard about life groups and had several invitations to visit different ones. The welcome we received meant so much to our family in those first fragile weeks of settling into yet another new place.

This also brings to mind missionaries who have returned from the field on furlough or who are about to head out into the field. Perhaps you have an extra room to offer? Several of my missionary friends have shared stories with me of the ways others have extended hospitality to them. Even though I may not have known the person or family offering their home or a room, my own faith was encouraged by the generosity of others.

As I think about meals I have prepared for guests or recall times my family have been guests, the memories spill over. Yes, there was good food and drink, but mostly I remember the contentment and joy I felt.

It was a joy our Lord shared with his disciples. After Jesus's resurrection, he appeared to many of his disciples before he ascended to heaven and the gospel of Luke recorded one of these appearances. Two of the disciples were walking to the village of Emmaus when Jesus, unrecognized by them, came alongside. They discussed the events of the last several days. When they approached the village, the disciples urged "their companion" to stay and eat with them. He did. "When he was *at the table with them*, he took the bread and blessed and broke it and gave it to them" (24:30, emphasis added). The disciples looked at each other and exclaimed, "Did not our hearts burn within us" (v. 32)? How wonderful when we experience hospitality in such a way that we *know* God is present. When we practice hospitality, we experience God's love and care firsthand even as we are Christ's hands and feet caring for others. Jesus is embodied in physical form as we reach out to new people, care for friends, and as others reach out to us. Don't wait to practice hospitality until the house is remodeled or your student loan is paid off. Begin by inviting others into your home—be it a basement suite, "fixer-upper," or dream house—with what you have to offer *now*. What matters most to someone is the invitation. Someone sees me. Someone wants me. Someone cares about me. God has faithfully provided for all our needs and many of our wants. When we extend his love and grace to others, we draw closer to our Heavenly Father. We see him revealed through the practical act and heart attitude of welcoming others.

FOR FURTHER REFLECTION

1. Think about a time when you were the recipient of hospitality. What did it look like? What made you feel cared for

and loved? Thank God for the gift of hospitality and the person who extended it.

2. What makes you uncomfortable or fearful about hospitality? Why? Pray and ask God to remove your hesitations and fears. Decide to take a first step in practicing hospitality and invite someone into your space.

3. As I mentioned in this chapter, food and hospitality are inherently linked. One of the best pieces of advice I was given about hospitality was to develop a few "entertaining" menus that I could easily prepare. I have two. These menus have saved me numerous times. They are favorites with my own family and with others. If you have never considered this approach, try it. What recipes do you prepare well? Make them your "go-to" dishes for guests.

MENU 1 (VEGETARIAN)

Manicotti
Salad
Corn
French Bread
This Manicotti recipe came from my Aunt Karon via my mom. I have made it countless times and have never been disappointed.

> 1 pkg. manicotti shells
> 1 16 oz. container ricotta cheese—I use part-skim ricotta.
> 1 pkg. (16 oz.) mozzarella cheese—grated
> 1 pkg. grated Romano cheese—no substitutions! Parmesan does not have the "bite" of Romano. The cheese is a key part of the dish's overall flavor.

2 eggs

1 pkg. frozen, chopped spinach—thawed
and drained

1 large jar Prego® traditional spaghetti
sauce—Yes, Prego® it is. The sweetness of
this sauce compliments the flavor of the
cheese. I have tried other jarred sauces
and been disappointed with the results.
You can also make your own sauce, of
course.

Slightly cook the manicotti noodles (approx. 4–5 minutes).
Drain. Mix together the remaining ingredients except for the
Prego. Stuff into the noodles. (This is the most time-intensive
part of the recipe.) Pour a thin layer of Prego on the bottom
of a 9 x 13 pan. Arrange the stuffed noodles in the pan. Pour
the remainder of the sauce on top of the noodles. Sprinkle
with some of the mozzarella cheese. Cover with foil and bake
at 325 degrees for 1 hour.

MENU 2

Chicken Marbella—pronounced *Mar-BAY-ya*
Salad
Roasted Vegetable
French Bread

This recipe came to me from my dear friend, Jacquelyn. The
recipe originally appeared in *The Silver Palate Cookbook* by Julee
Rosso and Sheila Lukins.[20] All I can say about this dish is,
"Wow!" This recipe is for 10 to 12 people because it is such
a wonderful dish to serve for a party. It can be doubled. It is
equally delicious served hot or at room temperature, so it is
great for a buffet or picnic, too.

4 chickens, 2 ½ pounds each, quartered—I
generally use thighs and drumsticks because I think dark meat has the best flavor.
You can also use chicken breasts.
1 head of garlic, peeled and finely pureed
¼ c. dried oregano
coarse salt and freshly ground pepper to
taste
½ cup red wine vinegar
½ cup olive oil
1 cup pitted prunes
½ cup pitted Spanish green olives
6 bay leaves
1 cup brown sugar
1 cup white wine (red wine works fine too)
¼ cup Italian parsley or fresh cilantro,
finely chopped

In a large bowl combine chicken quarters, garlic, oregano, pepper and coarse salt to taste, vinegar, olive oil, prunes,
olives, capers and juice, and bay leaves. Cover and let mar-
inate, refrigerated overnight. Preheat oven to 350 degrees.
Arrange chicken in a single layer in one or two large, shal-
low baking pans and spoon marinade over it evenly. Sprinkle chicken pieces with brown sugar and pour white wine
around them. Bake for 50 minutes to 1 hour, basting frequently with pan juices. Chicken is done when thigh pieces,
pricked with fork at their thickest, yield clear yellow (rather than pink) juice. With slotted spoon transfer chicken,
prunes, olives and capers to a serving platter. Moisten with
a few spoonfuls of pan juices and sprinkle generously with
parsley or cilantro. Pass remaining pan juices in a sauceboat.
To serve Chicken Marbella cold, cool to room temperature

in cooking juices before transferring to a serving platter. If chicken has been covered and refrigerated, allow it to return to room temperature before serving. Spoon some of the reserved juice over chicken.

BOOKS (AND A MOVIE) ABOUT HOSPITALITY AND ENTERTAINING

Over the years, I have collected a number of books that approach the topic of hospitality and entertaining well. Here are some of my favorites.

The Barefoot Contessa cookbooks, Ina Garten—Ina's food budget may be larger than most of ours, but her no-nonsense and "real" approach to food and entertaining is refreshing and helpful. Her recipes are straightforward and consistently good. At the end of many of her cookbooks, she has prepared menus listed. As Ina often says, *"How easy is that?"*

Bread and Wine, Shauna Niequist—Shauna's hope is that you will read this book, "turning corners of pages, breaking the spine, spilling red wine on it and splashing vinegar across the pages." My copy fits this description. Each chapter begins with an essay and ends with a recipe. Shauna gets food and hospitality. Read this for inspiration and to understand more deeply the sacramental nature of sharing a meal around the table with others.

My Homemade Life, Molly Wizenberg—Molly is another writer who marries essays and recipes beautifully. She is the author of the award-winning blog Orangette. Her relaxed style and delicious recipes makes you want to head to the kitchen and start cooking.

The Spirit of Food: 34 Writers on Feasting and Fasting Toward God, Leslie Leyland Fields, editor—These diverse writers share their hearts, faith, recipes, and their spiritual practices of encountering God at the table and in creation. This book is a rich, theological treatment of food and faith.

Open Heart, Open Home: The Hospitable Way to Make Others Feel Welcome & Wanted, Karen Mains—Karen's solid, theological understanding of hospitality is woven throughout this practical book. Readers will appreciate her honesty as well as her creativity.

Living on Less and Liking it More, Maxine Hancock—Maxine's book isn't about hospitality, per say. She writes about her family's experience of suffering a major financial blow and how they survived, even thrived, during a difficult season of life. Yet even when finances were lean, the Hancocks practiced hospitality, sharing what they had with others. Threads of hospitality and welcome are woven throughout her story.

Christian Reflection, Hospitality, The Center for Christian Ethics at Baylor University—This is a good study for a small group wanting to explore a more thoughtful, theological approach to hospitality. Many of the contributors are seminary and university professors.

Babette's Feast—This 1987 Danish film is directed by Gabriel Axel, based on the story by Isak Dinesen (Karen Blixen). Set in a remote 19th century Danish village, two pious sisters agree to take in Babette, a refugee from Paris, as their housekeeper even though they cannot pay her. Babette consents. Unexpectedly, Babette comes into a large sum of money from a lottery ticket that she renews yearly, her only connection to her former life in Paris. Taking all of her winnings to prepare a meal for the sisters and the villagers, Babette prepares a once-in-a-lifetime feast that proves to be an eye-opening event for all.

Encountering God in Rituals

> Louisa was slow and still in her movements; it took her a long time to prepare her tea; but when ready it was set forth with as much grace as if she had been a veritable guest to her own self....Louisa had a damask napkin on her tea-tray, where were arranged a cut-glass tumbler full of teaspoons, a silver cream-pitcher, a china sugar-bowl, and one pink china cup and saucer. Louisa used china every day—something none of her neighbors did.
>
> —Mary Wilkins Freeman, "A New England Nun"[21]

Steering the car into the driveway, I breathed a sigh of relief. It was Friday, the end of another workweek. The weekend was here. Jacob and Anna grabbed their backpacks and lunch boxes, heading inside the house. Within minutes, school clothes were cast off and play clothes were donned. I crashed on the couch for a quick nap, hoping for a "second wind" to sustain me until bedtime. As I dozed off, the thought of "what's for dinner?" flitted across my mind. A small groan escaped my mouth. Then I remembered it was Friday. Another sigh of relief washed over me. Dinner was under control. Homemade pizza was on the menu tonight.

This weekly ritual connected my family with each other and with God as we gathered around the table. That's the beauty of ritual. It provides a structure and a comfort to everyday life.

RITUAL: WHAT IS IT?

Part of what makes me "Alicia" is that I become really excited about new beginnings. A new school year, a new season, a new year—all of these fill me a sense of anticipation. One of my regular New Year's Resolutions is to read through the Bible in a year. I find myself flying through the pages of Genesis and Exodus, caught up in the unfolding story. Then I hit a wall in Leviticus. Chapter after chapter explains *in detail* the protocols and procedures for the Israelites in regards to sacrifices, offerings, and festivals. What happened to the compelling narrative? Filling the pages of this book are the rituals God wants his people to follow. Rituals that will bring forth repentance, thanksgiving, and worship. Leviticus is *the* handbook for following God's law. Later, when Jesus arrives on the scene, the Jews want to know, "What do we do now? Follow the law or follow you?" Jesus explains, "I have not come to abolish [the law] but to fulfill it" (Matt. 5:17). Jesus patiently explains to his followers, "These rituals you have done for hundreds of years pointed you to me. They served to remind you of your need for me in all aspects of your life."

Those rituals were essential for deepening faith and trust

in God. The Jewish people knew them intimately because they practiced them over and over. This is true for us as well. Anytime we want to learn something new, we practice... a lot. In this process of repeating and reviewing, the ritual becomes a part of our heart, mind, and soul, permanently engrained in our being.

A ritual is an act or a series of acts done in a particular situation and in the same way each time. Merriam Webster says, "always done in a particular situation..."[22] I often interchange the words "routine" or "habit" because these two words capture much of the same meaning, the regular, repeated way of doing something. I am drawn to the word ritual, however, because it suggests an integration of the spiritual life with the rest of life. Susan Schaeffer Macaulay, the daughter of Francis and Edith Schaeffer, wrote a book called *For the Children's Sake*, in which she talks about the importance of routines and habits, especially for children. We can benefit from her advice whether we have children or not: "Routines form habits. They are frameworks we can think about. We can make priorities."[23] She goes on to say that routines are especially important in the context of human relationships. They provide the frame upon which we can hang our experiences. They can be the narrative structure of our stories. In my own experience, eating dinner together is a given. From my earliest memories of childhood, gathered around the table with my mom, dad, and brother, to my own family, first Brad, and then our children, eating supper as a family is something we do. This is part of my story—the pausing and sharing of a meal most nights of the week. If this wasn't a priority, I can't imagine how many opportunities I would have missed for conversation and a sense of togetherness. In my family's life, mealtimes are one example of the "framework"

Macauley describes. I need to tell you that by nature I am a routine person. I *love* them. My life has an order and rhythm to it that provides stability and a structure so I can function well as a human being. I feel better when I follow my daily routines. When I have a couple of days without any sort of regularity, I become irritable and grouchy. Guess what type of person I married? You guessed it. Someone who doesn't love routines nearly as much as I do and can sometimes chafe under the "restrictions" my habits impose on the rest of our family and on him. Brad does recognize the importance of routines, and he appreciates the way they support our family life. But he loves spontaneous adventures like setting up the tent on a cool fall night and sleeping outside with the kids or bundling up and walking outside in the middle of a heavy snowstorm while the rest of the neighborhood stays hunkered down inside. You can see the rub here. My desire for following a routine can quickly give way to an inflexible rigidity and can feel suffocating to our family life if it is only about following the routine and not caring about the person or situation in the moment. On the other hand, never having a set time to eat dinner or to go to bed can lead to confusion, uncertainty, and a sense of flying by the seat of our pants. As with most situations in life, there needs to be both balance and flexibility. Regardless of your wiring, maintaining certain rituals is important whether you are married, married with children, or single. Different families will have different routines, but rituals enrich all of our lives because they can become a way to experience God's presence more intentionally as we live out each day.

RITUALS: WHY ARE THEY IMPORTANT?

When Jacob and Anna were younger, the times when I would leave home for a few days to attend a retreat or a work conference, or to visit a friend were a big deal. Dad was in charge. Before I left, I would write down menu suggestions and each day's schedule. You can probably guess the response I received when I came home. Brad: "Thank God, you're home!" My children: "Mommy's home!" While it was fun to have dad in charge for a few days, forgoing some of the usual routines, everyone was ready to return to "the normal pattern." Rituals are important because they establish familiar rhythms and routines, no matter what season of life we may find ourselves in. Rituals aren't just for families. They are for everyone.

RITUALS GROUND US TO REALITY

Our culture gives us glimpses of unreality all the time. From Pinterest to Instagram to the covers of popular magazines, we are constantly bombarded by unrealistic images, convincing us that everyone else's circumstances are better than ours. Advertisers spend millions of dollars telling us we deserve a designer wardrobe or house renovation or that we should buy the very latest in coffee-making technology even though our current coffee machine serves out a brew which is just the way we like it. Whatever it may be, the language is basically the same: "you need this" or "you deserve that" or "THIS will make you happy." How do we zero in on what is true and thus ground ourselves in reality? By spending time in God's word and by engaging with the people in our life face-to-face, and both of those in ways that deepen with repetition over time.

We don't have to look very far to recognize that life is hard. As much as we may long for life to be one wow moment after the next, most of life is mundane and ordinary. For some, your life is not what you expected it to be. Finances are tight, your to-do list never ends, you are butting heads with your spouse, child, mother-in-law, or best friend. Perhaps a health issue is nagging at you or depression regularly stands on your doorstep. Exhaustion, sadness, or just plain old irritation can leave us vulnerable to the temptation of drinking another glass of wine at night or enjoying the flirtatious comments of a coworker. Reality and rituals tether us to the truth and remind us of God's presence and involvement in our lives, even in the midst of difficult circumstances.

For the first year Brad and I were married, I was completing my student teaching in order to graduate from college. We were living in Van Wert, Ohio, at the time and I drove to Ft. Wayne, Indiana, each day for my student teaching assignment. I left our apartment a little after six am Monday through Friday. Most of my hour-long commute was in the dark. As excited as I was to become a teacher, this was a hard and challenging season in my life. Each day I came home exhausted physically and mentally. I felt stretched thin due to the demands of lesson planning and managing high schoolers. I needed some life-giving rituals during this season of life, but I was young and immature, unaware of my own needs in some respects. Instead, I gritted my teeth and slogged through this period, counting down the days until my student teaching ended. Fast forward five years to a scene in Glen Ellyn, Illinois, where I was a new mother. As much as I loved my new baby, hearing Jacob's hungry cries in the middle of the night when my body craved sleep sometimes felt like more than I could manage. Sitting in the darkened nursery, I wondered if

I would ever sleep more than a four-hour stretch.

I realized I needed some new, supportive rhythms if I was to survive this intense period. I joined a local MOPS group (Mother of Preschoolers) that met every other week, which became a bi-weekly ritual for me. Spending time with other mothers reassured me I was not alone and undergirded my commitment to mothering well.

RITUALS PROVIDE MEANING
AND SIGNIFICANCE

Rituals can be a vessel to hold the essence of who we are or a measuring stick that delineates the boundaries of what is important to us. They give meaning and significance to our lives. This is especially crucial when our emotions feel dead or dull and we don't feel like doing something. Many of my friends who worship in traditions that follow the church calendar or are liturgical in nature echo this sentiment. When life's irregularities are too hard and it is an effort to attend church, it is a freedom and comfort to follow the liturgy for that particular Sunday. Their worship experience isn't dependent on their emotional wellbeing that day. The scripture passages and the prayers give a framework to worship and create a space to meet God weekly, regardless of whether you're liturgically minded or not.

Weddings and funerals are another example. When we gather as friends and family for a wedding, we are witnesses to the vows spoken and we celebrate and affirm the beginning of a new life together. We come face-to-face with God's goodness that, as the Psalmist describes, "follows us" (Psalm 23). Likewise, when we gather together to mourn the loss of a loved one or a friend, we talk together, we eat together, we share memories with one another, we acknowledge God's goodness and mercy even as we sorrow. The horrible bewilderment of grief is tempered by these familiar rituals.

When my grandfather passed away, I saw aunts, uncles, and cousins I hadn't seen in several years. We reminisced about Grandpa during our time together. I recognized God's presence and compassion as we gathered in this way, thankful for the promise of heaven.

Rituals serve as markers or guideposts along the path of our life. Life is more than a series of days in the week, month, or year. We need the daily reminders, the weekly reminders, and the extraordinary reminders to point us toward God and the fact that he cares about all of it—big or small.

RITUALS: WAYS TO ENCOUNTER GOD

My evangelical upbringing remains a significant part of my faith journey. I am grateful for this heritage. Throughout my teenage years and even into college, most retreats or camps I attended spent a sizeable amount of time discussing the importance of "daily devotions," the "quiet time," or "personal Bible study." Sitting in my seat, with furrowed brow, I furiously scribbled notes in my journal and resolved to "do better" in regards to my devotional life. Whenever I reread my journals, I both laugh and groan at how harsh I was on myself when I missed a day (or more) of reading the Bible or praying. My thinking about personal piety didn't allow for much grace then.

Perhaps some of the speakers could have softened their message to sound less legalistic; however, I am grateful for the emphasis placed on daily devotions, which did develop into a habit for me as a young teenager.

This habit was sorely tested during the years my children were young and waking early. Each night I had the best of intentions to get up and read my Bible and pray before the kids woke. Yet when the alarm went off, and it was dark and the bed was warm, the last thing on my mind was Bible reading. I wanted sleep! Later on, as I went about my day, guilt and discouragement set in by another failed attempt. Sound familiar? I wish I could say I found a way to make regular Bible reading and prayer happen during those young-mom years. I didn't. Whenever I have a chance to speak to young mothers now, I tell them to be gracious with themselves. God isn't keeping a scorecard. But where does that leave us? Do we give up and say it is too hard? Is there some middle ground? I believe there is, but it still requires building a habit on our part.

PRACTICE THE CHRISTIAN LIFE

I referenced Tim Keller's sermon series "Practicing the Christian Life" in my Hospitality chapter. I like this phrase because it captures so well what we must do: *practice* the Christian life. Bible reading and prayer aren't going to become easy for me because I want them to. I have to practice at it. I have to work at it, which means moments of success and moments of failure. Instead of allowing times of failure to turn into extended periods where we fret or stew about failing yet again, we need to recognize our finitude and imperfection. We just need to plug along! It is hard to keep practicing at something that doesn't always come easy. Prayer takes real *work*. More often than not, I find myself daydreaming about what I plan to wear to work that day or worrying about a difficult conversation I had, and I forget what I was praying about in the first place. Bible Study takes real work. But there are those moments, and great spiritual figures and everyday, ordinary people like you and me have experienced them too, when we see God in a fresh way in the pages of Scripture or we hear him speak to us. This usually happens unexpectedly and quite unannounced, and if we hadn't been practicing at Bible reading and prayer we would have missed it altogether.

Technology provides helpful resources for our devotional times. I have a Bible app on my phone, for instance, making it possible for me to read my Bible anywhere. *The Book of Common Prayer* is online too, which follows the lectionary reading for the year and provides a structure for daily devotions. If you prefer to listen to the Bible read, many apps offer this option as well. An acquaintance of mine finds that the rhythmical movement of knitting while listening to the Bible quiets her mind and allows her to listen and pay attention better. What one person does for a quiet time may look totally different for another person. That's okay! And a good time for you to read your Bible may be a horrible time for someone else. Nowhere does Scripture say that the only time to have personal devotions is in the morning. As with establishing any habit, it may take some time to figure out what works best for you. Feel free to experiment as well as to start small. I know that when I become excited about a new idea or a new plan, I tend to set the bar really high. As with establishing any habit, make your initial goal achievable—go for ten minutes of Bible reading daily (set your phone alarm!) rather than thirty. And what if you think you don't have room in your schedule to be still before God, reading his Word, listening, and praying? If developing a deeper relationship with God is a priority, it may well mean giving up some less important call on your time.

KEEP A PRAYER NOTEBOOK

One ritual that I stumbled upon during the years I was a homeschooling mom was to keep a prayer notebook with my children. Each morning before beginning school, I would ask Jacob and Anna what they wanted to pray about and then we would write our requests in the notebook. I dated each entry and then we prayed. I also kept track of answers to prayers. These notebooks are a lovely record of those several years and clearly show God's hand in our lives. One prayer request that was especially significant to me was the selling of our home in Elgin, Illinois. I mentioned before I was often anxious and fearful, waiting all those months. I wearied of writing the same request day after day. I longed for the moment when I could write, "The house sold!" Eventually it did, and it was a happy day for me on April 21, 2004, to write those words.

I learned a great deal about faith as a result of that experience, and so did my children. Through the ritual of writing our prayer requests and praying together each morning, we saw firsthand how God provided for our family. My children learned that they could pray about things serious and things lighthearted. Most importantly, they saw that God does answer prayer. Not always on our timetable, but he does answer prayer. If prayer is a challenge for you, try a notebook. Incorporate the practice in a way that suits your own life or your family's life.

As you seek to encounter God through Bible reading and prayer, take comfort from the words of Paul in 1 Timothy 1:14. Paul says, "the grace of our Lord overflowed for me." Later in the chapter he says the events of his own life occurred so that, "Jesus Christ might display his perfect patience." We all need the promise of God's grace and patience with us as we try to incorporate Bible reading and prayer into our everyday lives.

MEALTIME RITUALS

Mealtime rituals are important for all of us, and God is certainly present at the dining room table! Mothers of young children, hang with me here. I can still recall the dinners where I ate cold food and did not complete a single sentence the entire meal. Sitting around the table with my children was not a highlight of my day. Now, my two young adult children have schedules of their own, and the challenge is to find a time when we can all eat together! The main encouragement I have for those of you with young children is to start early and to not give up. Yes, there will be moments when sitting down as a family for dinner feels like a complete waste of time. Everyone leaves the table cranky and disappointed. Keep at it! Children learn through routine and habit, and eventually there will come a time where everyone stays seated in his or her chair, no food is spilled, real conversation happens, and you find yourself thanking God for the people around your table.

One of the chapters that continues to inspire me and give me ideas in Edith Schaeffer's *The Hidden Art of Homemaking* is simply entitled "Food." Schaeffer understands the importance of good food and taking the time to sit down and enjoy conversation. Can you imagine how boring food and mealtimes would be if God had created pills for us to take instead of real food? No sourdough bread. No strawberries. No crème brulée.

One of the aspects I love about Schaeffer's approach is

that she isn't encouraging this ritual only for families. If anything, she speaks quite strongly to those who may have empty
nests or who are single. Why should those without children
not sit at the table to eat? Do you take time to actually set the
table? What if you are single? The temptation is to not even
cook, but to grab a sandwich or eat a bowl of cereal for dinner. Edith and I would both say "No!" Be intentional in this
area. Invite a friend to join you for dinner once a week and
cook a meal together for the occasion. It could be your weekly
ritual. If it is your spouse and you eating dinner, put away the
smartphones while you eat. These moments of talking and
eating together connect you to each other, and to the Creator
who made us with a desire for relationship. Before you eat,
offer a simple prayer of gratitude for the food on the table.
This act instills in us an openness to all the ways God provides
for our needs.

While we lived in Vancouver, we had several sets of friends
who lived in community houses. These were homes where
five or six people lived together to share the cost of renting.
One of the parts I envied about this arrangement was that
once a week, on a set night, they would gather together to
share a meal. I admired the way they connected with one
another despite their busy and different schedules. Many of
the small groups I have been a part of included eating dinner
together at least once a month. If you peeked in the window, you would have seen young and old represented around
the table. What a beautiful reminder of what God's kingdom
looks like.

If you have young children who are still learning the art of
sharing about their day, try the ritual of a High/Low Report.
Each person shares something good about the day or something that wasn't so good. This simple exercise provides an

opportunity for each family member to share and allows for follow-up questions. After busy days spent apart, our hearts are reset to God and a fresh understanding of how he cares about the details that are important to us, whether momentous or trivial, sad or silly.

At the beginning of this chapter, I mentioned Friday night homemade pizza. Part of what makes this ritual work in my family's life is an easy pizza dough recipe adaptable to a minimum 20-minute rise or a longer one-hour rise. I also appreciate this ritual because I don't have to think about it, especially at the end of a workweek. You may think this sounds counterintuitive. However, my whole self knows exactly what to do, even if I am on automatic pilot, and when I am too tired to think about what is for dinner, at least I don't have to think on a Friday night! When my daughter was younger, she was often by my side, helping me make the dough. This weekly ritual is our family's way of ushering in the weekend and thanking God for another completed workweek. Rituals provide purpose and value—even something as simple as homemade pizza.

Another food ritual my family enjoys is "Snicky-Snack Sundays"—a term coined by my daughter. This ritual gained traction in my family's life because it was something I was already used to. As a young girl, my family did not eat a "normal dinner" on Sunday nights. Instead, we ate our big meal after church. Sunday nights were for popcorn, a bowl of cereal, sliced apples and cheese, or a taste of something "leftover." Somehow the ritual stuck. True confession: we've had more than a few weeknight dinners where the menu was "Snicky-Snacks," bonding together while forgoing strictly balanced nutrition, as an exception to the general rule! Be creative and have fun with your mealtime rituals.

One last mealtime suggestion is to light candles. Why save the candlesticks for company or special occasions? This simple act sets the dinner hour apart from the rest of the day's activities. When I no longer worried that one of my children might set the house on fire, both Jacob and Anna enjoyed the chance to light the dinnertime candles. Find a mealtime ritual that will work for you. It doesn't have to be fancy. Allow your ritual to serve as a vehicle for recognizing God's regular provision in your life and to thank him for his presence.

THE WEEKLY RITUAL OF WORSHIP AND SABBATH

Providing a framework for our personal and family rituals is the weekly corporate ritual of worshipping God together. The opportunity to come together physically as the Body of Christ to worship and praise the living God is a wonderful privilege for believers. I know what it is like to rush around on a Sunday morning, herding everyone out the door to get to church on time. Frazzled emotions and exhaustion make it difficult to fully engage in the worship service. However, if we can pause and focus our attention on God and remind ourselves of his presence, we can meet him during this time. Which leads me to observing the Sabbath. In today's fast-paced society, where the rhythms of work and rest often blur, this topic is important. God instituted the practice when he created the world. We aren't machines. We are finite human beings and we need to weekly recharge and rest. Yet how often do we do this?

Over the years I have struggled at times with guilt or disappointment regarding my Sabbath practices. Some weeks are better than others. Sometimes I really do have to finish the laundry or grade school papers because of unforeseen circumstances. A helpful question I have learned to ask myself is, "Do I need to do this right now?" Often, if I slow myself down to answer the question honestly, I realize the task can wait. This simple question gives me clarity and frees me to enjoy the rest that the Sabbath affords. It is also helpful to consider Sabbath preparation. What do I need to do *now* so that I can really rest on the Sabbath? Perhaps this means I work harder on Saturday in order to make this happen.

And Sabbath-keeping should *not* be boring! As a child, I felt like Sunday was the longest day of the week. My dad was a pastor, so Sunday afternoons were for naps and reading the newspaper. To an active eight-year-old, nothing could be duller. The irony is that as an adult I love Sunday afternoon naps!

The Sabbath is a great day to spend time with family and friends. Pack a picnic when the weather is nice and enjoy creation by taking a walk or visiting a park. Read a good book. Play a game. Depending on your work schedule, you may need to pick another day of the week to observe the Sabbath. If you want to read more about Sabbath-keeping, I recommend a couple of books at the end of the chapter that have helped shape my thinking.

SEASONAL RITUALS

Finally, I want to point out that there may be rituals we engage in periodically—retreats or practices we observe for a period of time. For instance, two of my friends planned a spiritual retreat for themselves. They set an agenda that included times of solitude, times of prayer, times of discussing a book they wanted to read together, times for walks, and times for fun. Both of these women are mothers to young children and balancing both work and home responsibilities. This retreat was a key time of refreshment for both of them and a chance to connect with God very intentionally. In recent years, a group of women in my community have taken an overnight retreat during our school's Spring Break. We eat together, pray together, sing together, and have a mini-curriculum we follow during this twenty-four hour period.

At one of my former churches, the pastor would take one day a month as a day of solitude. This day was key for him to get away and hear God speak. When I lived in the Chicago area, a close friend hosted a "silent retreat." A group of 20-something women gathered at her house for a 24-hour period and were silent. It was a bit surreal at first, especially eating dinner together in complete silence, but we embraced this period and sought to hear God's voice in the quiet. We ended our time by sharing a pancake breakfast and talking about what we had learned. Seasonal rituals can be the "out-of-the-ordinary" experiences that give us fresh perspective and fresh energy for our faith journey.

Lastly, if you are part of a church tradition that doesn't follow the church calendar, or if you have gotten away from it, you may find this meaningful in your personal life. Observing the cycle of the church year—Advent, Christmas, Epiphany, Lent, and Easter takes a person through the gospel every year. What is missed one year is picked up the next, creating opportunities for church-season rituals as well as providing needed repetition, which instills a sense of anticipation. At the end of the chapter, I include a helpful resource if you are looking for ways to make Advent or Lent, for example, more meaningful in your life or your family's.

Homemade pizza on Friday night looks different for my family these days. Our weekly ritual has changed to adapt to our life at a boarding school. And that's okay. Most Friday evenings find my family eating dinner in the dining hall during the school year. Homemade pizza has moved to Saturday night or Sunday night, depending on the week. Certain routines will come and go based on our life's circumstances. New rituals are established. Don't be intimidated to experiment with individual or family practices that support and strengthen your walk with God. Enjoy the process of figuring out which rituals remind you of God's presence in your everyday, ordinary life.

FOR FURTHER REFLECTION

1. Think about a routine or habit that you perform most days. How can you encounter God as you move through that routine? It may be that you decide to pray while you wash those dinner dishes. It doesn't have to be "big," but find one way to increase your anticipation of God's presence in an everyday habit.

2. Are your personal devotions feeding your spiritual hunger and slaking your spiritual thirst? Can you write your name in the dust on the cover of your Bible? Do you feel as if you are "going through the motions" whenever you read the Bible or pray? What steps do you need to take to build and develop your personal devotions into a more regularly joyful part of your life? Think about one or two small starting places that could make this a more vibrant point of daily, nourishing contact with God.

3. We all need to eat. And eat well! Reflect on your current mealtime practices. Are there some rituals you could incor-

porate into the dinner hour that would make it more satisfying?

Below is the "famous" pizza dough recipe that saved me many a Friday night. It is now permanently seared in my memory.

Pizza Dough—Jonni McCoy, *Miserly Moms*[24]

Makes one large pizza.

> 1 c. warm water
> 1 pkg. dry yeast (2 tsp.)
> 1 tsp. sugar or honey
> 3 c. flour (I often use 1 cup wheat flour and
> 2 cups white flour.)
> 2 Tbsp. olive oil
> 1 tsp. salt

In a bowl, mix the yeast, sugar and water, stirring to dissolve the yeast. Let the mixture rest for 5 minutes. Add the remaining ingredients. Knead the dough on a floured board, adding more flour until the dough isn't sticky. Don't add too much flour or the dough will be become hard. Place dough in a bowl and cover, letting it rise from 5 minutes to 2 hours, depending on the texture you want your dough. Punch down the dough and shape into a large pizza. Top with your favorite combinations. A favorite in my family is Canadian bacon and mozzarella, sprinkled with goat cheese. I usually add some chopped vegetables on half of the pizza—red pepper, tomato, broccoli, or whatever I have on hand. Bake at 450 degrees for 15 minutes.

RECOMMENDED READING ABOUT THE SABBATH

Keeping the Sabbath Wholly: Ceasing, Resting, Embracing, Feasting, Marva J. Dawn—When I read this book, I breathed a sigh of relief. Sabbath-keeping didn't have to be dull! In fact, it was so much more than "going to church," which Dawn says is "bad theology." Recognizing the whole person as she writes, Dawn explains, for instance, that ceasing is more than not working. It involves the mind and heart too. Am I ceasing from worry and anxiousness as well? This is a must-read if you want a holistic understanding of the Sabbath.

Sabbath: Finding Rest, Renewal, and Delight in Our Busy Lives, Wayne Muller—Muller's book gave me permission to practice a Sabbath afternoon or a Sabbath walk or a Sabbath hour, even if I couldn't have an entire Sabbath day. This encouraged the rule-following nature in me. I have many friends who start their Sabbath on Saturday evening and end it late afternoon on Sunday. As a teacher, I find I often need Sunday evenings to prepare my lessons and myself for the coming week. Muller's book gives the reader a variety of creative ways to renew and refresh while observing the Sabbath.

Let Us Keep the Feast: Living the Church Year at Home, Jessica Snell, ed.—While this book doesn't address the Sabbath per se, it is a helpful resource for understanding the church calendar, which will in turn affect your Sabbath-keeping practices. Here's a brief explanation about the book: "Written for Christians who want to embrace the historic traditions of the church, and whose desire is to bring them into their daily lives and homes, *Let Us Keep the Feast* seeks to provide explanation, guidance, and resources for richer, fuller practices for living the Church Year at home."

OTHER AUTHORS WHO WRITE ABOUT THE SABBATH

Eugene Peterson—While Peterson doesn't have a book specifically about Sabbath-keeping, this topic frequently pops up in his many books. He gets the practice and I often find myself thinking, "I want to spend a Sabbath with him." In addition to practicing the Sabbath well, he lives a life that reflects meeting God in the ordinary. One of his titles that I have read most recently is *Practice Resurrection: A Conversation on Growing up in Christ*. The book takes the reader through Ephesians and is worthy of a slow, meditative reading.

Kathleen Norris—Like Peterson, Norris doesn't have a book devoted to the Sabbath. Yet sprinkled throughout her works are suggestions and helpful ways of thinking about this practice. I found *The Cloister Walk* to be particularly meaningful. In this book, Norris writes about her experience at a monastery and living with Benedictine monks for a period of time. Sabbath-keeping was a central part of this experience. The reader will appreciate her insights and observations.

Encountering God When Spiritually Adrift

> My dear Wormwood, I hope my last letter has convinced you that the trough of dullness or "dryness" through which your patient is going at present will not, of itself, give you his soul, but needs to be properly exploited....Let him assume that the first ardours of his conversion might have been expected to last, and ought to have lasted, forever, and that his present dryness is an equally permanent condition.
>
> —C.S. Lewis, *The Screwtape Letters*[25]

The days of having young children at home are behind me. Jacob is a college student and Anna will graduate from high school soon. I marvel at the reversals in our schedules. Most days find me waking up to a quiet house, and at night, I am the one who is in bed before the two of them! When they were infants and toddlers, I wondered if this time would ever come. My young children drained me physically, spiritually, and emotionally. Believe me, there are days when I would trade the teenage issues of dating and independence and angst for dinner-table temper tantrums in a heartbeat. But I do relish the new luxury of waking up slowly and savoring my morning coffee. No one needs me to feed them, bathe them, or dress them.

It seemed an almost cruel twist of fate that during my most intense season of motherhood, finding time and energy to connect with God was such a challenge: I knew I needed to spend time in God's word and pray, and yet I struggled to do it. My mom friends echoed the same sentiments: for them, too, parenting infants and toddlers stirred up a storm of hindering crosscurrents. Spiritual challenges and hardships can come at anytime, and I am not implying that spiritual drifting only happens to mothers of young children. Not so. I learned about how exhaustion can create a sense of distance from God during my children's early years. But, whatever season of life you're in, feeling alone and distant from God is painful.

Periods of highs, middles, and lows are the reality of the Christian life. Many of us find ourselves in a middle period most of the time, seeking to be faithful in the ordinary routines of life. At some point, however, most Christians experience a low point—a dry spell—a drifting—where God feels distant, even inaccessible. What precipitates this scenario varies. Perhaps it is the result of a personal tragedy. Perhaps it is suddenly feeling that for months you have been only "going through the motions" in your Christian walk. Or perhaps it is the recognition that your faith has been marked primarily by questions and doubts, and you wonder how much longer you can hang onto belief in God. Discouragement becomes your norm.

I have walked through seasons of uncertainty and difficulty in my own journey. I have also experienced God's peace and presence in tangible ways. But my norm isn't warm fuzzy moments with God. I read my Bible. I pray. I daily seek to be mindful of the Holy Spirit's work in my life.

Truth be told, if I based my faith on whether or not I *felt* God's presence regularly, that side of my faith ledger would look skimpy. I don't doubt his presence, but I don't experience a tangible feeling either. Where are you as you read this chapter? I ask, because writing about aimlessness in our faith walk is, frankly, intimidating. I have friends who have been wounded deeply by trite phrases or quick fixes applied by fellow Christians. The last thing I want to do is to gloss over the pain and disappointment you may be experiencing. Each of our faith journeys are personal and nuanced. Even though my story may look different than yours, a follower of Jesus has a wealth of truth at her disposal, including the wisdom of others who have walked through times of spiritual dryness, to teach us what it means to find God in the dark places.

And what about the role of suffering? Spiritual emptiness and suffering are often linked. Where is God in the midst of my suffering? Why doesn't God reveal himself to me when I read his word and talk to him? The truths discussed in this chapter apply to your situation whether you are spiritually adrift or in the midst of hardship. Recently a friend reminded me that for the Christian, suffering isn't meaningless. He said we believe that God is the Redeemer of *all*, including the times we feel rudderless and the times of suffering. How God chooses to redeem and restore the circumstances of our lives is part of the mystery, wonder, and grace of each of our journeys. We accept that sometimes, this side of heaven, we won't have the answers to our questions. Yet as Christians we always have confident hope.

SPIRITUALLY ADRIFT: WHAT IS IT?

My Long Island residence is less than a mile from the water. One of my favorite walking routes takes me right by the Sound. No matter the time of day, I can witness the tidal landscape changes. Occasionally, I notice some flotsam in the water. This floating debris represents what I think it means to be spiritually adrift—aimless, directionless, at the mercy of the elements. The feeling "I'm not even sure how I got here." These empty times confront us with the disconnect between what we *know* to be true and what we feel. Our minds tell us that God is near, affirming the words we read in Scripture. Yet, in our hearts it appears that God is unreachable, no matter how often we ask to feel his presence.

When I was in college, it was popular in my Christian circle to evaluate one's spiritual life in terms of whether you were currently "spiritually dry" or "spiritually fed." Sitting in a dorm room, my friends and I would share how we were doing. The dry metaphor popped up frequently, each of us constantly rating our spiritual health. In hindsight, I am not sure this was not the most helpful activity. We indulged in a bit too much navel-gazing—dwelling on the quality of our "quiet times" instead of seeking to live faithful to Christ in the everyday twists and turns of our studies and relationships. Sometimes the cure for our spiritual dryness is the cure I wish I could have given my college-age self: "Go work, Alicia. You'll feel better once you're being active." But sometimes the dry times are much more profound than the mere listlessness of immaturity. Sometimes it has nothing to do with our own virtue or lack thereof. Sometimes our hearts aren't merely a suburban lawn that hasn't been watered in a week. Sometimes the drought feels as severe and long-lasting as the cataclysmic changes that formed the vast desert plains of the Sahara.

If you are in a season of spiritual dryness, take comfort. You are not alone. Christian heroes of the faith such as Augustine, Martin Luther, C.S. Lewis, and Mother Teresa have written about their search for God in the midst of darkness and strife. The pages of the Bible are filled with stories of real individuals calling out to God in times of distress and loneliness. I particularly love the Psalms because they capture the highs, middles, and lows of David's life with God. The Psalms have been called the prayer book of the church. If these ancient songs show us how we're supposed to talk to God, then we can take it as given that we're allowed to be honest with him. We're allowed to confess just how horrified we are at our own fear and despair. We're allowed to not just praise and laugh, but to beg and plead and wail. God already knows the truth of how we feel; it is good for us to admit it, with words, in his presence. David's joys and cries echo our own joys and cries.

SPIRITUALLY ADRIFT: WHY IS THIS TOPIC IMPORTANT?

In the middle of John's Gospel, while eating the Last Supper, Jesus prepares his disciples for his final hours on earth. In chapter 16 he tells them, "In this world you will have trouble. But take heart! I have overcome the world" (NIV). Jesus' plain-spokenness here is refreshing. He isn't trying to hide the fact that his followers will struggle. Whether you find yourself new to faith or a seasoned veteran, hardship will come. Knowing this ahead of time can soften the element of surprise. Immediately after Jesus tells his disciples about the inevitability of trouble, he follows up his comment with an assurance: "But take heart!" Experiencing spiritual dryness doesn't have to be a death sentence to our faith. God's presence is with us. He has overcome the world. His love and care for us, as well as for our circumstances, has not and will not change.

LEARN TO WALK ALONGSIDE OTHERS

One of the many poignant images in the *Lord of the Rings* trilogy is the faithfulness of Sam as he travels with Frodo to destroy the ring of power. In the final book, *The Return of the King*, the burden of carrying the ring becomes almost too much for Frodo. Hungry, thirsty, and tired, the two hobbits trek on, determined to fulfill their mission. Frodo, now almost consumed by the ring's power, fluctuates between moments of lucidity and irrationality, believing at times that Sam seeks the ring for himself. Yet Sam remains faithful. He continues on with his friend to the very end.[26] The ability and willingness to come alongside a friend in a time of need is a true gift. When our faith journey becomes too difficult and Bible reading and prayer seem impossible, we need someone like Sam to travel with us.

This concept of walking alongside our friends also appears in Scripture. When God allows the devil to test Job, three of his friends show up.

> Now when Job's three friends heard of all this evil that had come upon him, they came each from their own place, Eliphaz the Temanite, Bildad the Shuhite, and Zophar the Naamathite. They made an appointment together to come to show

him sympathy and comfort him. And when they saw him from a distance, they did not recognize him. And they raised their voices and wept, and they tore their robes and sprinkled dust on their heads toward heaven. And they sat with him on the ground seven days and seven nights, and no one spoke a word to him, for they saw that his suffering was very great (Job 2:11–13).

If you have read the story, you know that while Job's friends start off well—mourning with their friend, sitting with their friend, being silent with their friend—they eventually say some stupid things while trying to explain the cause for Job's suffering. We can learn from this too. Our desire to say the right thing or fix the situation can lead us to say untruths or to resort to unhelpful clichés. Simply being present and alongside our friends can be more helpful than our words. Often, listening well can be more helpful than responding.

In Preston Yancey's book, *Tables in the Wilderness, A Memoir of God Found, Lost, and Found Again*, he writes about a Christmas when God felt particularly absent. Despite the distance he felt towards God, he headed to the Christmas Eve service at his church. A close friend who was heading into his own Christmas service several states away texted Preston saying, "I'll keep watch for us."[27] That's what friends do. They walk alongside us, encouraging us, praying for us, and challenging us when the road is too difficult to walk alone.

DRAW CLOSER TO GOD

I know this sounds counterintuitive, but times of spiritual dryness can also be times of deep growth and insight. At different points in my life, and especially when God has felt distant, I have prayed "God, I need you to show up. I need you to make yourself known to me." In those instances, I hoped for a "big reveal." I wanted to be wowed by God's awesomeness and splendor. The reality is I have never had this particular prayer answered by a "big reveal." Instead, my prayer has been answered in small, nondescript acts such as watching my children play, or noticing a vivid sunset, or eating a peach so sweet and juicy that I smiled with delight. Almost unconsciously I found myself thanking God for his goodness and I realized his presence was there with me that moment, as it had been all along.

Even more comforting, God accepts our scraps of faith in order to draw us closer to him. Jesus tells his disciples, "If you have faith as small as a mustard seed, you can move a mountain" (Matt. 17:20 NIV). Have you ever seen a mustard seed? I actually held one in the palm of my hand during a church service. I couldn't believe this tiny black fleck could become a huge tree. Earlier in Matthew's gospel, Jesus references the mustard seed in a parable: He says the birds can perch on the tree's branches because it is one of the garden's largest plants. Something small, like our faith, can grow in surprising and unexpected ways if we are willing to step towards God. Trusting that he will meet us, even in the dark times, can feel uncertain and risky. Yet unless we move towards God in faith, we will never know how he can use the lonely, difficult place to grow us and draw us closer to himself.

REAP THE BENEFITS OF OUR HABITS

In my chapter on rituals, I talked about the importance of habits and routines as they form the bedrock for our human experiences. When we trudge through the shadowy valleys, our spiritual habits can sustain us even when we feel like a spiritual fraud. We draw from our well, sometimes very deeply from our well, and are refreshed with the truths of God's unchanging attributes. When I am physically tired, hungry, or thirsty, I lose my ability to think clearly and rationally. Just ask my family. All it takes is for one thing to go wrong and suddenly I am on a downward spiral. Thankfully, I have a husband who reminds me that before I declare that everything is horrible and my life stinks, I should suspend my opinion and go to bed, eat some food, or rehydrate. (Or perhaps all three!) It is the same spiritually. We take a wrong turn, lose our way, and become discouraged. Our healthy spiritual habits guide us back to God's truth and reality. Our spiritual disciplines of Bible reading and prayer lead the way into listening to God, worshiping Christ, and breathing the Holy Spirit in and out. We look up and see that he is, indeed, leading us on level ground (Ps. 143:10) and that the way is lit (Ps. 119:105).

SPIRITUALLY ADRIFT: WAYS TO ENCOUNTER GOD

As human beings we tend to isolate ourselves when we are suffering or in pain. Being vulnerable or admitting our lack of control is scary. Of course, the irony is that this is precisely when we most need others. They also help pull us away from an inward focus and remind us to seek God's loving presence.

FIND FRIENDS AND FELLOWSHIP

In chapter four, I mentioned the role MOPS played for me as a young mother. I was the first one in my group of friends to have a baby. My closest friends worked full-time jobs, and it was a challenge to get together with them regularly. I needed to know I was not alone in my thoughts and feelings as a new mom. My church did not have a MOPS group so I took the initiative to find a local group at another church. Walking into the church's lobby for the first time with my baby in tow took courage; I felt like I did on the first day of school—nervous, expectant, wondering if anyone would talk to me. Thankfully, the smiling moms at the registration table welcomed me and enfolded me, which made being a newcomer easier.

Attending MOPS primarily met a social need for me, but it also fed me spiritually. It wasn't an inductive Bible study, but I encountered God's grace and presence in this bi-weekly gathering of moms. I was reminded of God's care for me, my children, and my spouse. I saw God's goodness displayed in the women caring for the children and in the women making delicious food for me to enjoy. These women traveling on the same part of the Motherhood Road as I was on buoyed me up and carried me along through an exhausting and wonderful season. What a blessing and encouragement to be not alone!

PRAY WITH A TRUSTED FRIEND

During the years my family lived in Waco, I prayed regularly with a dear friend. Our lives shared many similarities: both of our husbands were working on PhDs, we both worked full-time jobs, and we both had school-aged children. Margaret and I poured our hearts out to each other and to God. We both felt stretched thin at times and there were times when it felt like too much to meet up, but we needed each other and this sacred space where God gathered together with us. Often we didn't have answers or suggestions for each other, but that didn't prevent the prayers going up. If God feels remote, approach a trustworthy person in your life with the request to pray together. Praying in twos doesn't flip a magic switch and suddenly you feel spiritually fed and watered. But over time, you will together witness God's presence and answered prayers. As your hearts are forged and shaped through this, you will enjoy the deep blessings of intimate spiritual companionship with both God and your praying friend. "Iron sharpens iron, and one [woman] sharpens another" (Prov. 27:17).

CHANGE VERSUS ACCEPTANCE

What if you have felt spiritually becalmed in the doldrums of life, seemingly without even a holy puff of the air from the Spirit, for months, even years? A Christian friend who is a licensed therapist taught me the importance of recognizing the concept of change versus acceptance in our lives. We live in a change culture. If you don't like your house, you change it. If you don't like your job, you change it. We even have the opportunity to change our physical appearance! But what happens when you can't change your circumstances? This is where acceptance enters the equation. Some Christians live their entire lives wrestling with doubt and aloneness. Nothing about their Christian walk is easy. I don't know why some struggle more than others. It seems unfair and I want to ask God, *why*? When I go to the Bible to look for answers, I find the character of Jeremiah.

Jeremiah did not have a pleasant life. The biblical scholar Charles Feinberg says Jeremiah's life "may be characterized as being one long martyrdom."[28] Throughout the book, it was Jeremiah's job to warn Israel of her impending destruction if she didn't turn from her wicked ways. He relayed message after message, but they fell on deaf ears. In addition, Jeremiah spent time in prison; was beaten; was thrown into a cistern filled with mud and left there for a long time; and even wore dirty underwear for a while before God told him to bury it and later, to dig up the underwear. *Really?* Jeremiah didn't hold back in telling God how he felt. He complained to God repeatedly about his people, their evil ways, and their lack of repentance. At one point he said to God, "Why did I come out from the womb to see toil and sorrow and spend my days in shame" (Jer. 20:18)? Despite Jeremiah's messages from the Lord, the Israelites did not repent. He witnessed the capture of his people and the fall of Jerusalem. Yet reading through this book, I find a prophet who loved the Lord deeply and remained faithful to his task. Many scholars agree that Jeremiah was the most Christlike of all the prophets. Their stories were similar. Both knew the meaning of loneliness. Both shared an unusual fellowship with God. Their honesty and openness with God about their feelings and thoughts is a model for us all.

In my own life, I have struggled to embrace the acceptance piece of this equation. My natural temperament is to do or to fix. Acceptance feels passive. Yet, in reality, this is the farthest thing from the truth. Acceptance requires *faith*. Faith to believe that Jesus overcame death and rose from the grave. Faith to believe there is a heaven. Faith to believe that God does not rejoice in evil and does not ask us to pretend that evil is good, but promises to completely restore us and his created world in the end. Faith to trust in the Lord and his goodness, in spite of any suffering we receive from his hand.

I have felt the acceptance rub most keenly in my marriage. As much as I love my husband, we are two different individuals. He likes to stay up late; I like to go to bed early. He likes to eat something sweet a couple of hours after dinner; I like to eat dessert right after the main course. He prefers to focus on one task at a time; I prefer to switch back and forth between several tasks. He thrives on deadlines and does some of his best work crunching a time limit; I like to work at a project over time, chipping away at it bit by bit. Even after a quarter of a century of marriage, I still struggle with wanting to change my husband and make him more like me.

During our years of living in Waco, the demands of Brad's graduate degree, my full-time job, and raising two children exacerbated our differences. Frustrated, angry words spilled out of my mouth more frequently. I knew a bitter seed threatened to take root in my heart and it scared me. For a couple of years, Margaret, my praying friend, and I prayed the same prayer: "Lord, help me to love Brad well, supporting and encouraging him rather than being critical."

God has been faithful to us, teaching us how to communicate with one another and learning to love each other better, differences and all. Our temperaments will never change! Learning to accept that "my way" isn't the "better way" is likely something I will struggle to accept until "death does us part." On the other hand, I am willing to learn to yield as God trains we two to be one.

RECEIVE FROM GOD AND FROM OTHERS

On several occasions, I have been caught "unawares" by a knock at the door from a friend who either showed up a bit early or unannounced. Standing there in my yoga pants and sweatshirt, with bedhead and no makeup, I feel exposed and uncomfortable. In those moments, as much as I may want to shut the door and say, "Come back in an hour when I have a chance to clean up," I need to let go of my desire to present a "put-together" image. This is not easy. Learning to receive from God and from others when we are not just unprepared but beyond that, we are unable to do anything on our own, requires humility and a willingness to admit we are not in control. Can we receive what God has for us in that moment? Can we allow ourselves to receive from others when we have nothing to offer in return?

This is a hard one for me. I pride myself on my organizational skills and my ability to juggle responsibilities and multitask. The more I accomplish in a day, the better I feel. In the last trimester of my pregnancy with Anna, our family moved to our first home in Elgin, Illinois. I loved this 100-year-old house for its leaded-glass living room window, high ceilings, and crown molding. The house also needed a lot of work! Frustrated by my lack of mobility and flagging stamina, I sat on my couch looking around at all the projects that begged to be completed. I had difficulty letting go of my expectations for how I wanted my house to look *right at that moment*. Adding to my frustration was the limited budget and time we had to work on these projects. I spent far too much emotional and physical energy focused on my unrealistic expectations rather than on God's blessings and provisions—friends who helped us move and paint, a healthy pregnancy, the gift of a house, to name just a few. I look back now and know that I missed an opportunity to gratefully receive these blessings from God and others, and to give him the glory.

When I think of learning to receive, I think about Mary, my mother-in-law's dear friend. Talk of Mary came up often at family gatherings in the early years of Brad's and my marriage. Marva, Brad's mom, was Mary's close friend. Mary suffered chronic illness and encountered multiple near-death experiences over the twenty-five years of her sickness. I often wondered how she was still alive. Her health issues were numerous and complicated. The astronomical health bills weighed heavily on Mary's family. Early in the friendship, Mary's husband, Carl, would tell Marva and others, "We're fine," not wanting to receive any help. It took months for him to realize this group of friends wasn't going anywhere and they were determined to help. Listening to these stories, I marveled at God's miraculous provisions for Mary and her family time and again. Lying in a hospital bed, hooked up to numerous machines, there was no way Mary could give Marva or her friends anything. While Mary may have been frustrated at times by her inability to "return the favor," I know that for Marva, her faith grew as she witnessed God's care and love for Mary. Learning to receive is a gift we not only give ourselves, but also a gift we give to others.

A "danger" of being a Christian for most of my life is that I sometimes tend to gloss over parts of Scripture that are familiar to me. One early memory of Sunday School includes the story of God freeing the Israelites from slavery in Egypt. You probably know the story, too. For 400 years, the Israelites lived as slaves, enduring many hardships. I imagine there were countless times when God's people wondered if they would ever see deliverance. Eventually, God called Moses to be the one to take his people to the Promised Land. Once the Israelites left Egypt (in a pretty miraculous fashion if you ask me) you would think the process of settling into their new homes would have happened fairly quickly, but it didn't. For 40 years *after* the Israelites leave Egypt, they wandered in the desert because they failed to trust God that they could defeat the inhabitants of the Promised Land, even though he explicitly told them the land would be theirs. During these years of difficulty and hardship, God refined and deepened their faith and dependence on him. In spite of the Israelites' disobedience and rebellion, God was the ever-faithful shepherd to his people. He even gave them a visual reminder of his presence—a cloud by day and a fire by night for their journey.

I know how quickly I begin to complain or despair when my circumstances are difficult. I want resolution, not waiting! When I reflect on the demanding years of raising young children or I recall the times when God felt distant, I wish an actual cloud or ball of fire led me like it did for the Israelites. Surely, then, I wouldn't doubt God's nearness! But, if I'm honest, I'm afraid I would react like the Israelites, creating my own idol or rebelling in some other way. So whether I feel God's presence or not, I trust that his promises are true and hold fast to them.

God is my ever-faithful shepherd, too. His Word is a visible reminder of his presence. I experience the nudges and affirmations of the Holy Spirit. I belong to a company of other believers who walk alongside me on the way. God is near.

FOR FURTHER REFLECTION

1. In the section on why this topic is important, I explain that times of spiritual dryness can teach us to learn to walk alongside others, to draw closer to God, and to reap the benefits of our habits. Which of these points resonated with you or needs growing in your own life?

2. When you have felt spiritually adrift, what has been the biggest hindrance for you in recognizing God's presence? Why do you think this is so?

3. For centuries, many Christians have prayed the Psalms.

These prayers have a way of echoing our heart's cry. Consider taking the next couple of months to read a Psalm a day (or more if you are so inclined). In my own life, as soon as I finish reading the Psalms, I start over, making Psalm reading a regular part of my quiet time. You may even want to jot the date or a detail about your life next to the Psalm you read to serve as a marker. If you are a person who hates to write in books, you can use a journal. For instance, next to Psalm 63, I have the date July 11, 2007, and the words "Lake Michigan" written next to, "I have seen you in the sanctuary" (v. 2), which reminds me of the beauty of God's creation. Over time, these dates and written notes are a testimony of God's presence in my life.

ADDITIONAL READING

Knowing that we are not alone when we struggle is a comfort. Many faithful Christians have written about their experiences in spiritual memoirs. Some of you may be familiar with St. John of the Cross. His name often pops up in conversation when talking about feeling spiritually adrift. Check out his poem "The Dark Night," and see why Christians throughout the ages have found comfort and hope in his words.

Below are some additional recommendations. There are *many* more books out there. If you have already read these, ask someone you respect for some new titles.

Faith and other Flat Tires, Searching for God on the Rough Road of Doubt, Andrea Palpant Dilly—This book is Andrea's story of finding her way back to God. Growing up in a Christian home and the daughter of missionaries, Andrea walked away from her faith, disillusioned and filled with doubt.

Surprisingly, she found her doubts serving as a pathway back to God.

Traveling Mercies, Some Thoughts on Faith, Anne Lamott—With Anne's trademark humor and self-deprecation, she tells her remarkable story of finding Jesus. This book had me laughing out loud one moment and subdued and thoughtful the next. Anne tells it like it is—honest and real.

The Genesee Diary, Henri Nouwen—If I were to give the title of "spiritual giant" to anyone, I would give it to Henri. He had a deep faith in God. What makes his writing so refreshing is his ability to admit his faith struggles and his desire to get past himself. He feels like one of us!

God in the Dark, Through Grief and Beyond, Luci Shaw—I had the privilege of auditing a class taught by Luci when our family was at Regent College. This book is the story of her husband's terminal cancer and Luci's journey with him through his death and the first months of widowhood. She doesn't shy away from asking the hard question, "Where is God's promised presence?"

Surprised by Oxford, Carolyn Weber—Read this book and experience what good writing is! Carolyn's rich and thoughtfully crafted sentences are pure pleasure to read. In an academic world where faith is ridiculed or viewed as intellectually weak, Carolyn finds God and embarks on a journey of faith as a graduate student at Oxford.

Encountering God as a Caregiver

I've come to understand this caring work as a calling, one that continues to beckon. Seasons of life bring new incarnations, but caregiving remains a vital part of who I am. I've been captured by the truth that my life and work change the shape of people and their worlds. This makes it important work. And because it has such power, I take it very seriously.

—Andi Ashworth, *Real Love for Real Life*[29]

Growing up, I never heard my mom complain about staying home to raise my brother and me. I never heard her say, "I'm bored." I never felt like she was "biding her time" until she could return to the workforce. I observed a woman living a full and meaningful life, even though it didn't require a business card. She cared for her family, volunteered at church and school, practiced hospitality, and enjoyed creative outlets such as book club. She was a role model for me. She married my dad while still finishing her Bachelor's degree from Biola University. She supported him in graduate school by working a variety of jobs and then stayed home as a full-time mom. She continued to be involved in women's ministries and carried the title "Pastor's Wife" for a number of years. When I entered junior high, she returned to the workforce full time, first as a secretary and eventually as an Associate Vice-President for Advancement at Taylor University, earning her Master's degree in her fifties while juggling this time-consuming position. Her years of investing in the home front inspired me when I became a young wife and mother. She would be the first to admit that she wasn't perfect—who is? But, her example showed me that caregiving is a worthy calling and not one that needs a string of explanations trailing behind it.

Well before I met Brad, I knew that if I had children one day, I wanted to be at home with them. When Brad and I found out we were expecting, we made plans to this end. For starters, we chose to stay in our apartment rather than buy a house and have a mortgage requiring us to be a two-income family. This felt like a hard *sacrifice*, as I thought we needed a house in order to raise a child. We did look at a few, but by the grace of God avoided the potential disaster of purchasing an unaffordable home. I came to accept that Jacob, our new son, was oblivious to the fact of where he lived. What he needed was the secure *home* of our love and care. Our spacious two-bedroom apartment proved perfect for our growing family. I never could have predicted the path my role as a caregiver would take. It wasn't until my mid-thirties that I even had the vocabulary to understand that "caregiving" encompassed more, much more, than staying home with children. Caregiving duties orbit into our sphere of responsibilities over and over again throughout the seasons of our life, and I only saw a piece of this truth when I was a young woman. Child-rearing may follow sharing an apartment with roommates, and perhaps is followed in turn by balancing a career and home life, managing a houseful of children, and then maybe caring for an aging parent, an ill spouse, a dying in-law. In all of these times of burden-bearing, Christ's gentle presence and robust example beckons to each of us as caregivers.

As I look at my mom's life today, her role as a caregiver has changed. In recent years, her mother's declining health meant trips to California several times a year, taking turns with her sisters to spend time with Grandma, navigating the difficulties of caring for an aging parent who didn't live nearby. More recently, it meant that my mom put her life "on hold," often without much lead time, so she could be with her mother. It weighed on my mom that she didn't live closer to her mother, and it broke her heart when she heard my grandma say, "I miss my girls."

Yet my mom will be the first to say that she felt Christ's steadfast presence with her, even when this season felt like a bumpy rollercoaster ride. For each leg of this particular path, Christ's peace and strength have come just when she needed them most.[30]

SOME THOUGHTS ON STAYING HOME AND WORKING OUTSIDE THE HOME

As I write this, my oldest child is heading to college in a month. I can hardly believe how quickly the time has gone! I have all these memories of a little boy and then someone pushed the fast forward button and this young man is flex-ing his independence and a new level of autonomy. When well-meaning friends told me, "You'll blink and he will be out of the house before you know it," I was sometimes heard to mutter, "Yeah, right, it sure doesn't feel that way." But they were right. As my nest starts to empty out, hindsight and ex-perience clarify my thinking.

The season of staying home with my children (and it *is* a season) grew me in ways I could not imagine or anticipate. I would not be the wife, teacher, writer, and friend I am today without those life experiences. I chomped at the bit to speak and to write a book, without realizing I needed the crucible of life at home with little ones to develop and mature, to pre-pare myself to contribute to the larger conversation. While my children were growing up, so was I.

The early years of marriage and motherhood brought me face-to-face with my selfishness like no other period of my life thus far. I saw my pride and stubborn spirit in a new light. It was easy to point out Brad's faults, but to have him point out mine? Watch out! Suddenly, this sweet-looking girl dug in her heels and wouldn't budge on *anything*! Then the children arrived. My ordered world, which catered to my preferences and timetable, needed a major realignment. How could these two children, whom I loved so much that my heart ached at times, also cause me to feel such anger? And the fact that I could experience these two powerful emotions within a split second of each other really threw me for a loop. I cried out to God, "Help me, Lord! I don't want to be this way." Thus began—embarrassingly late—my long road of learning to die to myself. When I lost my patience with Brad because he wanted to have a plan first before heading into the city for an adventure, or when my "under-the-breath" comments at his impatience towards other drivers erupted into a fight, I sought forgiveness. When I yelled at my children for interrupting me for the umpteenth time while making dinner or for bickering with each other when they should be playing nicely together, I sought forgiveness. I continue to seek forgiveness from my family and from God. Even after all these years, I can still be the nicest, most stubborn person you have ever met! And yet, God's mercy and forgiveness meet me time and again. He has used the crucible of marriage and motherhood to refine me more into the woman he wants me to be.

In this way, the season of early married life and the season of staying home with young children grew me in important ways, making me a little more patient, a little more compassionate, and little more kind.

I recognize that not every woman who wants to stay home can. Financial realities may require both parents to work full time; even more true for the single mom or dad raising children alone. Some women feel *called* to full-time work. I have several sets of friends who equitably raise their children: while one spouse is working, the other is home with the children. This change about requires a certain level of freedom and flexibility, as well as some sacrifices, but they make it work. Some families flip the traditional model—dads can raise children full time, too! One of my colleagues is an excellent teacher. She works full time and her husband shoulders the daily child rearing responsibilities. Whether it is a shared role of parenting or one parent serving as the primary caregiver, every parent engaged in childrearing knows both the burden and delight involved in this type of work.

If you are in a season of staying home with children, know that *your work matters*. Tell yourself this truth every day because many in our culture will tell you otherwise. How grateful I am for the time I had to stay home with my children: the time to read them books, to take them on outings, to witness the myriad of childhood milestones. I did wish at times for more intellectual stimulation or adult endeavors, but when my wish came true and I had the opportunity to work part time, it proved more than I could handle, turning me into a stressed-out and grumpy woman. Anne-Marie Slaughter offers a refreshing view in her *Atlantic* article "Why Women Still Can't Have It All." Slaughter received her foreign-policy dream job at the State Department only to find that the demands of parenting her two teenaged boys caused her to rethink her long-held position on balancing career and motherhood:

> All my life, I'd been on the other side of this exchange. I'd been the woman smiling the faintly superior smile while another woman told me she had decided to take some time out or pursue a less competitive career track so that she could spend more time with her family...I'd been the one telling young women at my lectures that you *can* have it all and do it all, regardless of what field you are in. Which means I'd been part, albeit unwittingly, of making millions of women feel that they are to blame if *they* cannot manage to rise up the ladder as fast as men and also have a family and an active home life (and be thin and beautiful to boot).[31]

Staying home does not mean you must neglect your own interests and pursuits. It does mean you'll need to be creative about how you tend those passions, but don't lay them aside. A woman with a toddler in my community is an artist. She carves out time during nap-time to paint and draw. Sometimes she attends a Saturday art class while her husband fully engages with the children. When Jacob and Anna were little, Brad regularly encouraged me to attend book club or have a girls' night out with my friends, recognizing how important those times were to my emotional and mental health.

Consider how you portray this season of your life. Motherhood, although often challenging and even uncomfortable to be sure, is *not* the worst possible job on earth. But sometimes we mothers paint it that way. Instead of wasting your energy complaining, invest in supportive friendships with like-minded moms and pursue meaningful activities to enrich and refresh you. Hire a babysitter for a few hours occasionally or as a regular gig, and run errands or journal with a coffee, meet a friend for lunch or a walk, go to an exercise class or the art gallery, air out your mind and feed your soul. If your budget doesn't permit a babysitter, swap childcare with a friend.

Remember: "this too shall pass." Children grow up! I can now say, alongside all those older women who once said it to me: these years will be over before you realize. I used to wonder if my career would ever have a path again, or if romantic evenings with my husband would ever be unhampered by the babysitting expense. My circumstances have certainly changed. I now work a full-time job and no longer require the services of a babysitter. My experience has taught me that surprises—both good ones and hard ones—line each of our paths. None of these "surprises" catch God off guard, though. Trust in the Lord to provide for all your needs, and be prepared to be amazed at the ways he will care for you during this intense, ephemeral, valuable, remarkable season.

CAREGIVING: WHAT IS IT?

In my mother's generation, women who stayed home described themselves as "housewives" or "homemakers." Stay-at-home moms were the norm. The stay-at-home dad was an unknown. Nannies and other childcare options were not readily available. When I was home with my children, I referred to myself as a stay-at-home mom. I didn't have a problem answering the question, "What do you do for work?" except for the rare occasion when an uncomfortable pause followed my answer. Then I would suddenly feel small and insignificant, as if being at home with my children wasn't real "work." The term caregiving, however, indicates a broader understanding of the actual work of giving care. It is not limited to those who stay home to raise a family. I believe that all of us are caregivers.

Our relationships with others—coworkers, neighbors, family members, roommates, friends—require both our attention and our response. Caregiving encompasses the whole person, their physical, mental, emotional, and spiritual needs. Have you ever delivered a meal to a grieving friend? You are a caregiver. Have you ever done extra work on a project to help out a colleague? You are a caregiver. Have you ever listened to a hurting neighbor? You are a caregiver. I will always be a caregiver, even though my stay-at-home-mom days are over. The role of caregiver changes throughout one's life and requires flexibility and adaptation. My role now with my college-aged son is one of a listener and a sounding board for ideas rather than cruise director of his daily activities. Believe me, I'm still figuring this out!

CAREGIVING: WHY IS IT IMPORTANT?

The opening pages of Scripture tell the story of a relational God. After speaking a breathtaking creation into being, God fashions Adam from the dust of the earth. Knowing that he does not want man to be alone, God creates Eve, making both of them "in his own image" (Gen. 1:27). From the moment we are born, hard-wired into our DNA is the desire to be in relationship with others. To be known and to know. When we give care to others, we reflect the image of God. When I stop and consider this, all of the tasks I do to care for my family or others take on new meaning. Something as seemingly insignificant as washing my family's dirty laundry *matters*. Shoveling snow for an elderly neighbor *matters*. Helping a friend move *matters*.

When our family left the Midwest to move to Vancouver, BC, to begin our graduate school adventure, it was the end of 2003. As we drove across the country, we endured a blizzard, interstate closures, and *long* days of driving before we rolled up to our new home for the next couple of years. To say we were exhausted is an understatement. Our dear friends, Colby and Tammy, who drove with us, were also exhausted. Looking at our moving truck filled with all our belongings in front of our new house, I felt like crying. How were we ever going to unload all of our stuff? Recognizing I was close to despair, the guys sent Tammy and me, along with the kids, to grab some lunch. Sitting in the Subway, my phone rang. It was Brad, telling me that a friend of his brother's, who lived nearby, along with her husband and three teenaged children, had showed up to unload our truck. Words cannot describe the relief and joy I felt in that moment. By the time we returned from lunch, over half of the truck was unloaded.

God's care for our family was embodied in the Pianki family and their help in our time of need. Over the next several years, we were the recipients of their care and friendship on many occasions.

DEMONSTRATING WORTH AND DIGNITY TO OTHERS

Those who clean up others' messes as part of their job are in a unique position. Most people do not clamor for this type of work. Yet if we have ever been the recipient of this type of care, we are grateful for those who do it. Caregiving is important in that it gives worth and dignity to the other. Even more noteworthy is the person who does this job and treats the other with respect. When my children were infants and toddlers and they became sick, cleaning up messes moved to a new level. There are the normal, everyday types of messes that parents take care of on a daily basis. Then there are the "sick child" kinds of messes. During times of illness in our home, my washing machine ran constantly and my bucket of rags and cleaning supplies remained close at hand. When I wasn't cleaning up a mess, I was comforting and cuddling my sick child. As they grew older and were able to talk, I recall a number of occasions when my children apologized for not making it to the toilet in time or for misdirecting the contents of their upset stomachs onto the floor instead of into the bucket I had provided. I always tried to reassure them that it was okay. I knew it was an accident. Even at a young age, their vulnerability in those moments was apparent. Extending grace and comfort kept their worth and dignity intact. When we give care to others, we have the opportunity to impart by our actions and our words the message "you matter." It is also a chance for us to reflect on the way God cares for us—the kindness he shows us as he "cleans us up!" The love we feel caring for our children this way gives us a little, tiny glimpse of the love he feels for us, even in our mess and our sin.

CAREGIVING IN THE BIBLICAL NARRATIVE

Turn to the pages of Scripture for encouragement and examples if you wonder whether caregiving matters. I referenced Martha in chapter three, but here is a woman who embodies a caregiver. The Bible doesn't give a ton of personal information about Martha, but we know that she has a sister, Mary, and a brother, Lazarus. We also know she owns a home in a village called Bethany. On several occasions, she cares for Jesus and his disciples by providing a meal and a place to stay. John's Gospel says that Jesus loved these three siblings, suggesting more than just casual acquaintances. Coming to the home of Martha, Mary, and Lazarus met some of the physical and emotional needs of Jesus and his disciples.

And, of course, Jesus himself models caregiving. Think of that lakeside morning after his resurrection. The disciples decide to go fishing one night but are unsuccessful. As the sun rises, Jesus calls out to them from the shore to ask if they have caught any fish. They tell him "no." He instructs them to throw their nets one more time and this time, when they do, the catch of fish is so large that their nets begin to break. When the disciples come ashore, they find Jesus preparing a meal for them, complete with a fire, some fish, and bread. After the meal, Jesus reaches out to Peter and restores him spiritually. Using a lamb as a metaphor, Jesus asks Peter three times if he loves him more than the other disciples. Each time, Peter answers, "Yes, Lord, I love you more." This scene is a beautiful testimony of care and restoration, and it is Jesus' physical care for his friends that sets the stage for the spiritual and psychological restoration Jesus intends to effect.

As our family's time in Waco drew to a close, we benefitted from the care of others in meaningful ways. No matter how well you plan and prepare, the final days of packing are exhausting and overwhelming. Sometimes I think stuff hides until the very end, and then when you open a cupboard it reappears and you wonder, "Where did *this* come from?" On one of our last nights in town, friends invited our family over for dinner. Walking into a home that wasn't filled with boxes and was pleasing to look at soothed my frazzled nerves. The meal was delicious too. Grilled steak, roasted corn, salad, bread, and good wine rounded out the menu. We talked and laughed, easing the pain of saying goodbye. A couple of days later, several of my dear girlfriends came to help me clean the house after the truck was loaded. As we sat on the bare floor afterwards, gratefulness filled my heart. These were women who had demands on their time; yet, they gave of themselves. Their presence and their help embodied love and care for me at a stressful and exhausting moment in my life.

FOR SUCH A TIME AS THIS

There have been times when I tire of hearing the phrase "for such a time as this" from the book of Esther, because it is trotted out too readily in Christian circles. As our society relies more and more on technology and being efficient, the art of caregiving suffers. I use and enjoy social media regularly, but it doesn't provide the face-to-face interactions that I need. Staying connected with friends from around the globe on Facebook is something I truly enjoy, but it is not the same as drinking coffee with a friend who is sitting across the table from me. I need those times where I can be real and vulnerable. And technology can't provide the physical touch that we need as humans beings. Researchers continue to publish studies that highlight the importance of human touch. It's not just children who need hugs; even adults need hugs regularly. Holding hands around the dinner table when saying grace, embracing a friend, and where appropriate, touching the arm or shoulder of an acquaintance, connects us physically to others, imparting a sense of care.

Then there is the efficiency piece. Caregiving doesn't follow a timetable and is often messy and unpredictable, which is the farthest thing from efficiency. Walking alongside a grieving friend may take months. Caring for an aging parent may take years. How we give care to others should look different for Christians. We minister Christ's love and care when we reach out to the hurting and downtrodden. Since moving to New York, this reality has struck me in a new way. Every time I visit New York City, I encounter someone in need. Whether it is a person begging for money in the train station or walking past a person who is clearly not mentally stable, I am confronted by the needs of others. I have struggled with what my response should be. Do I give money? Do I offer to buy the person some food or coffee? One idea that I have yet to try is to buy a box of granola bars before heading into the city. When I see someone in need, I can offer him or her a bar. I know that one box of granola bars is a drop in the bucket, but in its own way it communicates care. I still have a lot to learn about giving care to those on the fringes of society. I struggle with feelings of awkwardness and uncertainty at times, but reminding myself that the person standing in front of me is made in the image of God helps. Over the years, I have read my share of dystopian fiction. Every once and a while after finishing a novel I wonder, "What if this happens in our society?" What if we decide that the weak or the aged or the mentally challenged are no longer needed? Who will speak up on their behalf? Who will give care to those that society no longer deems useful? My first response after asking these questions is to say this will never happen. My prayer is that it never will and my actions can be an embodiment of the desire behind that prayer, doing what I can to care for those who live with insecurity, pain, or need. As a follower of Christ, I want my caregiving to include those beyond my immediate circle of family and friends. I want to pay attention and recognize that perhaps I have been placed in this particular place at this particular time to show Christ's compassion to the person in my path today.

CAREGIVING: WAYS TO ENCOUNTER GOD

In Andi Ashworth's book *Real Love for Real Life* she writes about a time when she put her caregiving urges on hold while taking some classes in St. Louis. Once she returned home, a day came where her son and daughter-in-law became sick. As she was preparing soup for them, she burst into tears, thanking God for this opportunity to help.[32] Here was an opportunity to express who she really was and to satisfy an inner longing. Andi's story may not resonate with you because caregiving doesn't recharge you like it does her, or because you are exhausted by your particular season of life. Or you might find yourself somewhere in the middle. You have days where you wonder if what you are doing matters and days where you catch glimpses of the eternal significance of your work. Regardless of your circumstances, calling to mind that "the steadfast love of the Lord never ceases; his mercies never come to an end; they are new every morning" (Lam. 3:22–23), provides encouragement and hope. Caregiving is demanding work. The promise of new mercies *every day* is real sustenance. Each day brings the promise of God's grace, given to us as needed, never ahead of time, but we go forward, trusting it's true. Each day offers a new opportunity to encounter God as a caregiver.

PRACTICING THE PRESENCE OF GOD

I was in college the first time I read Brother Lawrence's short book, *Practice of the Presence of God*. Since then I have read it several times and continue to find it helpful. No matter how you spend the majority of your days, opportunities to pray and invite God's presence into your situation occur regularly. I think caregiving and some of the repetitive tasks that tend to go with this type of work (i.e. washing dishes, laundry, cooking) particularly lend themselves to "constant prayer."[33] I am not referring to the kind of prayer where you sit down and close your eyes. Instead, I am talking about a simple sentence said out loud or in your mind such as, "Jesus, remind me of your presence as I prepare dinner," or "Lord, fill me with your love and patience as I care for…." These sentence prayers said throughout the day connect us to God. They invite God's presence into our caregiving. This is why I found Edith Schaeffer's book *The Hidden Art of Homemaking* so helpful as a stay-at-home mom. Each day, no matter how ordinary it was, became an opportunity for me to experience God's presence and to share God's love with my children. Jacob was my animal-loving, bug-catching kid. An image that is permanently etched in my mind is of a blonde-haired boy, in a squatting position, studying an insect or preparing to catch a frog. For a typically cautious kid, he showed little fear when it came to catching creatures of all sorts. Sometimes I wished for a little more fear as he reached for a snake! Each catch became an opportunity for the two of us to marvel over and discuss the variety of God's creation.

SAVORING THE MOMENTS

Both of my children went through an "art phase." On any given day, a fair amount of paper was used for drawing or painting. As soon as one picture was completed, they would reach for another piece of paper and start a new one. There was no way to display or keep all of the artwork. For a while, Jacob drew only pictures of sharks and Anna drew pictures of people with flat heads on top and straight hair. Occasionally, they would depart from their current art obsession and make a picture or card for me. I've kept many of these treasures and pull them out from time to time to remind me of this season in life. These notes also testify to God's goodness and care for me as a mother of young children. One of Anna's notes says this, "*Mom I luv you. becus you mad good biscus and you our my momy.*" (Translation: She loves me and she loves the biscuits I make.) I saved this particular note because it reminds me that something as simple as making biscuits communicates love and care to my daughter. In turn, I am thankful to God for my children.

Savoring the moments doesn't apply only to our children. I mentioned my Grandma Smith earlier in the chapter. My grandma's limited mobility excluded her from many activities, so when my mom visited her, instead of taking her on wearying outings, my mom asked Grandma to share her memories. Listening to these stories of a bygone era became an opportunity to know more about Grandma's life and to share good memories together. Mom also read Scripture to my grandma, participating in the rich tradition of gathering together as believers and experiencing God's presence through the reading of his word. These memories provide comfort to my mom and extended family now that Grandma has gone to be with the Lord. Likewise, if you find yourself in a season of caring for a sick loved one, your presence and the holding of a hand creates a space for you to pray and meditate on God's Word together while you offer the gift of yourself. There is no agenda, nothing to accomplish in these moments. In a day and age where we measure productivity by how much we can squeeze into every second, our presence is a gift in itself.

SPACE TO RECHARGE

As rewarding as caregiving may be at times—the hugs, the notes, the "I love you's"—it is also a practice that can drain and exhaust. Late nights chatting with company, early morning wake-up calls to care for children, cooking countless meals and cleaning up afterwards: it all quickly takes a toll. Resentment and bitterness soon squeeze in to take root in a caregiver's life. Finding time to rest and recharge is important. To assume it all depends on us is a dangerous line of thinking. We say, "If I don't do it, who will?" At the root of this sentiment is pride, often masked by concern and a desire to help. We take on a God-like role, which clouds our judgment as we alone try to determine what really needs to be done and who needs to do it. I once spoke with a missionary friend about how to juggle all the needs and demands I saw around *me* and about how I felt guilty if I said no to something. She told me that just because there was a need didn't mean that God was calling me to fill that need. I have recalled her words of wisdom many times over the years. This doesn't mean that there won't be times when our plates are too full and we feel stretched too thin. Yes, God may be calling us to take on additional levels of caregiving and responsibility, but only for a time. This period cannot continue indefinitely. There comes a point where we step away and care for ourselves. The first time I read the letters that Edith Schaeffer wrote to family members and friends about their ministry in Europe and the starting of L'Abri (these letters were eventually published into two books, *With Love, Edith* and *Dear Family*[34]), I was blown away by all she did in a single day. She seemed to have unlimited energy, working late into the night and rising early to prepare a delicious, from-scratch breakfast for her family. Sometimes I wondered if my faith was as committed as hers. She gave and gave and gave to others. In many respects, Edith's model of caregiving is an example for us all. However, I think she would admit that there were times when she needed to do less and pull away more to care for herself and her immediate family. What struck me as I read the letters is that when the family did leave their responsibilities at L'Abri, they really left. And they stayed away for a while. I'm sure part of this was due to exhaustion and needing time to recover. As Edith described these holidays, she recounted sweet times of fellowship as a family, times of meaningful Bible study and family worship, and times for walks and picnics together. Gradually, the empty cup refilled.

In Psalm 23, David paints a lovely picture of renewal as he describes green pastures, quiet waters, and refreshment to one's soul. In the dailiness of caregiving, it can be easy to forget about God's steadfast presence. "Self-care" isn't merely a buzzword in today's society. God created us with a need to rest and he commands us to do it. If you're finding your caregiving responsibilities are squeezing out time for God, and you are running close to empty, it may be a signal that you need to rethink your commitments. You need to ask yourself some hard questions about your role as a caregiver. Are your energy resources depleted? When was the last time you experienced joy or a sense of God's presence? Have you committed yourself to too much? Do you need to speak up and ask for help? Some of you may feel your backs are to the wall. You are the one caring for small children or the elderly parent. From sun-up to sun-down, you are the primary caregiver. You would love an occasional break, but finances are such that hiring a babysitter or other help is impossible. Relief of any kind may feel beyond reach. Don't lose heart. Talk with your spouse or someone you trust. Think creatively. Pray and ask God to sustain you in this difficult season. Reach out to a friend or family member. Walking alone when you feel overwhelmed and discouraged heightens the sense of loneliness and isolation. Call to mind the words of the psalmist from Psalm 55:22, "Cast your burden on the Lord and he will sustain you."

I know there were times when my mom was at the end of her rope caring for my brother and me. I remember a day when the house was a mess and despite my mom's request for help, I wasn't cooperating. Suddenly, tears filled her eyes and she escaped to her bedroom. Oh, the guilt that tugged at my young heart! I made mommy cry! Years later, as a grown woman and a mother, I look back on that memory with another layer of insight. Now I know what my mom felt because I have felt it. Caregiving is exhausting work. There are days when the tasks before us feel too much. Thankfully, Christ's words are true. We can cast our burdens on him. He will lift us up, support us, invigorate us, cheer us, and supply all we need.

FOR FURTHER REFLECTION

1. Think about the definition of caregiving: the work of anyone who gives care to another person. What does this look like in your own life? Who benefits from your care? Which particular part of caring for the whole person are you drawn to—the physical, the emotional, the mental, or spiritual needs of others?

2. I suggest that caregiving should include more than our immediate family and friends. How does this play out in your own life? Do you find it easier to care for people you don't know than those you do?

3. How easy is it for you to find time and ways to recharge in your role as a caregiver? Conversely, what makes it a challenge for you? Think about a time when you encountered God's presence as a caregiver. Recall that experience. Pause and thank God for this reminder.

4. At the end of the chapter, I list several personal questions for caregivers. Which one of these do you need to spend time thinking and praying about? Spend some time meditating on God's character. How does he care for you? Provide for you? Nurture, heal, and restore you?

5. If you want to dig a little deeper, revisit the story of the Good Samaritan. Some would say it is *the* story about caregiving. Although you are probably familiar, or even very familiar, with this Bible story, a rereading of it now (perhaps in a translation you don't normally read, like *The Message* or the *Good News Translation*) will teach and challenge you afresh as to how we are to be Christ's hands and feet in a needy world. There are wonderful illustrated children's books of this story. Consider reading the storybook together with a child in your life, not necessarily one you are a parent to, and using it as a springboard to discuss mercy and compassion as attributes both of God and of us as followers of Christ.

RECOMMENDED RESOURCES

Coping with Your Difficult Older Parent: A Guide for Stressed-Out Children, Grace Lebow and Barbara Kane with Iwrin Lebow—As the Baby Boomers retire and move into their elderly years, books and resources that address caring for aging parents become even more invaluable. Grace Lebow and Barbara Kane use their experience as clinical social workers to help adult children navigate the emotionally draining side of caring for one's aging parents.

MichaBoyett.com—I first discovered Micha and her writing from my writer friend Ed. He recommended I read her book *Found, A Story of Questions, Grace & Everyday Prayer* as her writing overlaps with topics that I write about as well. In 2015, she gave birth to a baby boy named Ace, who has Down syndrome. On her website, she writes about first learning that she would have a special needs child. A number of her posts explore this topic and include titles for parents, family members, and friends who want to read more. Caregiving has its challenges even in the best of circumstances, but caring for a special needs child adds another layer of hardship. Micha's honesty along with her good writing gives voice to the joys and heartaches for those who find themselves in similar circumstances.

Real Love for Real Life: The Art and Work of Caring, Andi Ashworth—Andi gets caregiving. This book is theologically rich as well as immensely helpful in understanding the many-faceted dimensions of caregiving.

The Hidden Art of Homemaking, Edith Schaeffer—I recommend Edith's book in the Creation chapter. In many respects, I could list her book under each of my chapters. However, the recommendation bears repeating particularly for this subject. Edith embodies caregiving and her book reflects that.

The Quotidian Mysteries: Laundry, Liturgy and "Women's Work," Kathleen Norris—The inside notation in this short book defines quotidian as: occurring every day; belonging to every day; commonplace, ordinary. What a perfect way to capture the many aspects of caregiving! Beautiful writing and praise for all that we do—from laundry to housecleaning—can be found in the pages of this book.

Encountering God in the Workplace

> Whatever you do, work at it with all your
> heart, as working for the Lord, not for hu-
> man masters, since you know that you will
> receive an inheritance from the Lord as a
> reward. It is the Lord you are serving.
> —Colossians 3: 23-24 (NIV)

My entrance into the work world began in high school. For
two summers, I worked for Child Evangelism Fellowship and
taught backyard Bible Clubs. In college, my summer jobs en-
tailed office work—answering phones, filing, and other cleri-
cal duties. My first "real" job was waitressing at a Pizza Hut
in Van Wert, Ohio. A typical Pizza Hut this was not, but a sit-
down restaurant with two dining rooms. I got to know some
of the regular patrons in the three months I was there; I even
learned some of their orders. Bill liked pan pizza with cheese
and pepperoni and Kim liked a side of garlic cheese bread
with her order. While my stint as a waitress was short, my
time at the Pizza Hut significantly influenced me.

The star waitress at Pizza Hut was Sue. She'd been there

for about a decade by the time she trained me. Here I was, a young college graduate, and Sue ran circles around me. Her work ethic was formidable and her memory for each customer's order was remarkable. The regulars loved her and would wait for a table in her section to open rather than sit elsewhere. I loved it when my shift overlapped with Sue's. Her enthusiasm and quick wit made the work fun. I also enjoyed the hustle and bustle of the busy kitchen. In the kitchen, pizza sauce and swear words flowed freely. At the end of a shift, sitting in the back room counting the night's tips, the haze of cigarette smoke hung heavy in the air. All of this was new to me as a fairly sheltered Christian young woman. I loved experiencing the "real work world." When I was hired to teach at the local junior high and about to move on, the staff congratulated me with a purchased cake. I was humbled and honored by their gesture. These were people I enjoyed working with and I valued the community I shared with them. Even today, when I drive through Van Wert, I can't help but think about my time at Pizza Hut.

Since my days as a waitress, I have worked in a variety of jobs, most of them as an English teacher to middle schoolers. When school is in session, my daytime hours are filled with teaching, grading, and planning. Whatever *your* tasks and duties are, your job also consumes the majority of your day. Is it possible to encounter God's presence in the midst of work, where deadlines loom along with difficult co-workers and hard-to-please customers?

WHAT IS THE WORKPLACE?

The workplace is where you work, yes?—where you spend a good chunk of your time each day and are paid for your efforts. But in today's economy, "where you work" is often more nuanced and less obvious. Many jobs offer the flexibility of working at home rather than in an office, and some jobs allow for both. Whether you close your house door behind you each day or not, whether you receive an income or put in volunteer hours, you do some type of work. Paul's instruction to the Colossians is to us, too: "*Whatever you do*, work at it with your whole heart, as working for the Lord" (3:23 NIV, emphasis mine).

My workplace is also where I live. I teach at a boarding school and my home is on campus. I eat lunch and dinner most days with middle and high school students. On Sundays, I worship with them at our chapel service. My workplace very much intersects with my home life. When I taught at a day school, I drove to school and then back home again, but my workday didn't necessarily end when I drove away from the building. Lesson planning and grading consumed a portion of my evening hours, and still does today. Many professions entail working after hours. Additionally, the demanding expectations of today's global economy combined with the increased use of technology has blurred the workplace boundaries. We can work virtually anywhere and 24/7. This raises some red flags.

As much as we may love our jobs, we are created for *more* than work, as women and men made in the image of God. Yes, our work can be good and rewarding, but it doesn't define who we are. God loves me whether I teach the perfect grammar lesson or if I lie on the grass and watch the clouds drift across the sky, "doing nothing." Regardless of what I "do," I have value and worth as one of God's creatures. We may need to ask ourselves some hard questions. Do I define myself by my work? When does my workday begin and when does it end? Do I maintain a healthy rhythm of both work and rest?

I knew very little about boarding schools prior to commencing my work here. They appeared in books I read or movies I watched but my personal knowledge was limited. Both Brad and I were captivated by the idea of living and working with young people. What a beautiful example of community! And with amazing benefits. We were told about meaningful conversations that happen around the dining hall tables and the joys of hanging out with students outside of class time. But we were a bit nervous, too, as we were also told that the demands of the job were not to be taken lightly. As faculty members to middle and high school students, we are "in loco parentis," in the place of the parent, to students ages 11 to 19, 24 hours a day, seven days a week. During the school year, we are *always* open and on call. In deciding to accept the faculty positions, we did our best to factor in that our time would not always be our own, and this has certainly proved to be the case. Yet, in spite of this stretching, how grateful we both are to work and serve in this community! The compartmentalization of work—in a specific place and completing all tasks there before returning home—is less and less our experience or expectation.

WHY IS THE WORKPLACE IMPORTANT?

According to Gallup, the average American works 47 hours per week, almost a full workday longer than the standard work week of 40 hours.[35] Many work for even longer. Sometimes we joke about being "married" to our jobs, as we may spend more hours there than at home. I don't want to keep my work separate from the rest of my life as a Christ follower, especially since I spend a large amount of time working. The Lord is Lord of all, including my job. When I arrive in my classroom, I don't flip an imaginary switch and become a teacher, leaving my identity in Christ standing in the hallway. The hours I spend crafting a lesson, grading papers, or discussing literature with my students are opportunities to glorify God by using the gifts he has graciously given me and by acknowledging his interested presence in my busy day. I am both a follower of Christ and an employee. My workday hours take on new and deeper meaning when viewed in this light. Indeed, all of life takes on new meaning when we acknowledge the Lord is over all.

WORKPLACE RELATIONSHIPS

I have been blessed in my professional endeavors to work alongside people who I genuinely like. Yes, there have been the one or two "prickly" people along the way who were irritating or annoying, but they have been the exception. Some of my closest friends, in fact, have also been colleagues and I don't take this lightly, knowing this isn't the case for everyone.

I told you waitressing at Pizza Hut was my "first real job." Well, actually, I had one job before Pizza Hut. I worked at Burger King for two days. It was awful. Brad and I married the summer between my junior and senior year at Taylor University. Brad had already graduated and was working as a youth pastor in Van Wert, Ohio. I had a few more courses and my student teaching to complete before I graduated. I didn't work during the school year due to my academic load. You might say we lived on love rather than money! The bank balance ran pretty low most months. After my Taylor graduation, I really needed a job, and I was without a teaching position. Feeling economically pressured and struggling with a lack of employment confidence, I jumped at the first opportunity: Burger King. The job was awful. I felt dehumanized by the cloud of distrust surrounding all the employees. Because the default reaction to everything from both management and staff was suspicion, I continually justified my actions as I completed each task. The management showed little interest in any of us on the staff. They didn't seem to consider us real people. Even without a wealth of job experience behind me I knew this was *not* the environment where I wanted to work. You can imagine how grateful I was for my time at Pizza Hut. The contrast between the two restaurants was sharp.

Of course, not all of us have the luxury of choosing a preferred work environment. I share my unhappy work story to point out that the people we work with can make or break a job, often more so than the actual job itself. It's not that my stint at Pizza Hut was without difficulties: I waited on rude customers, some waitresses shirked their duties while the rest of us had to pick up the slack, and certain managers scheduled only their favorite waitresses for the coveted Friday and Saturday night shifts. But just as my years as a stay-at-home mom grew me as a person, so my workplace relationships have shaped me. And the process is ongoing!

Over the years, several of my close friends have filled administrative and leadership roles. One of the common refrains when they discuss their job challenges is the roller-coaster ride of *dealing with people*. While the job itself may be demanding, by far the biggest difficulties stem from fellow employees. "So-and-so isn't happy about this. So-and-so doesn't work well with this person. So and so verbally undermines others." The list goes on. As you read this, do you immediately think of a colleague? It only takes one person to make an otherwise enjoyable job an agony. What would your coworkers say about you? Are they glad to work with you?

As Christians, our workplace relationships are a training ground for us. In Paul's letter to the Galatians he writes, "Bear one another's burdens, and so fulfill the law of Christ" (6:2). I think Paul would include difficult coworkers under the category of burdens. You don't have to eat lunch with a troublesome colleague every day, but you *do* need to extend to them kindness and care, and you certainly *don't* participate in workplace gossip about them (or, indeed, about anybody). If you have wronged or hurt that person, you make every effort to restore the relationship. Following Christ's law involves loving others, even (or especially) the ones who rub us the wrong way. I have learned to embrace Atticus Finch's advice to Scout in *To Kill a Mockingbird*. After Scout has a rough first day of school and an altercation with Walter Cunningham, Jr., she seeks the comfort of her father. Atticus wisely tells her: "If you can learn a simple trick, Scout, you'll get along a lot better with all kinds of folks. You never really understand a person until you consider things from his point of view.... until you climb into his skin and walk around in it."[36] Considering the particular circumstances of Mr. or Ms. Hard-To-Deal-With often gives us a new and better perspective, changing our irritation to empathy.

THE WATCHING WORKPLACE

The last ten years of my teaching career have been in Christian schools. I love the fact that I work with people who share a personal relationship with Jesus and that I can freely share my faith, and I don't take this situation for granted. I have worked in much different environments. I first started teaching at a public junior high school at age 21. Not only was I learning the curriculum and how to manage a classroom of eighth graders, I was also learning the relational dynamics of the "teacher's lounge" and how to mesh with fellow teachers and administrators. In this small community, it was quickly known that I was the "youth pastor's wife." Someone would offhandedly comment that he hoped he hadn't offended me with his language, or the laughing at a joke would die when I entered the room. I never announced to my colleagues, "Hey, I'm a Christian," but they knew. They watched me. They also included me and treated me with respect. When they invited me to Happy Hour, I went, drinking my diet soda and happy to get to know my fellow staff members better.

When Brad and I moved to Chicago, I worked for a while in an office and the fact that I didn't swear, didn't demean others, and didn't spend my evenings bar-hopping marked me as different. Again, I knew I was being watched. I squirmed when colleagues talked about "religious" people. Many of the oft-heard stereotypes surfaced in these conversations. Words and phrases like "judgmental," "hypocrite," or "trying to convert me," made me want to crawl under the table and hide. I did not handle every situation well or always have the just-right thing to say. In hindsight, I wish I had spoken up more, been more courageous. But also in hindsight, I recognize the solid impact of carrying Christ with me into the workplace not so much in what I said or didn't say, but in how I acted. My actions carried the most weight. I did my job. I followed through on my responsibilities. I sought to be kind and respectful. What I *did* caught the attention of my colleagues.

Sadly, I have worked in Christian settings where professing believers behaved in ways not readily identifiable with

Christ's example. Gossip circulated freely, job responsibilities were neglected, and critical attitudes threatened work relationships. The fact that we are sinful and living in a fallen world plays out at work, whether in a Christian or secular environment. None of us are perfect. But when we have chosen to walk with Christ, we have a responsibility to be an example, to be a living letter others can read (2 Corinthians 3:2–3). Yes, we will undoubtedly fail or react poorly, but those times can be redemptive. We accept responsibility for our actions. We apologize. We forgive.

As you reflect on your personal work history and I on mine, three principles come into focus. First, can we affirm that we have done our work "as working for the Lord?" Or do our colleagues see us cutting corners and leaving things undone? Second, are we building authentic, sincere relationships with our coworkers or are we merely politely tolerating them? They are not "evangelism projects," but real individuals made in God's image, with needs and concerns. When we listen well and show genuine, sustained concern, trust and rapport are established. Third, are we inviting the Holy Spirit to be our work colleague? We daily need courage, wisdom, and grace to fulfill our job duties *and* to be Christ's ambassador as we rub shoulders with others, some of whom may be hostile towards us because of our faith. Take heart and remember to pray as you navigate through your work day, knowing that God is also at work there even if we can't see what he is doing.

WISE AND WINSOME

Each day at work there is an opportunity, often many, to exercise wisdom. This is a given. Whether it is deciding if I should penalize a student for uncompleted homework or discussing a student's low test score with a concerned parent, I need wisdom. And that wisdom needs to be winsome. In a difficult and tense moment, the sarcastic response on the tip of my tongue threatens to increase the overall stress level; but the engaging, appropriate words I thankfully decide to use instead diffuse the budding animosity and direct the conversation into a more healthy exchange.

The book of Proverbs is filled with verses about wisdom and its source. "For the Lord gives wisdom," says Proverbs 2:6. A few verses later, it says the Lord is "guarding the paths of justice and watching over the way of his saints. Then you will understand righteousness and justice and equity, every good path; for wisdom will come into your heart, and knowledge will be pleasant to your soul; discretion will watch over you, understanding will guard you" (8–11). Our workplace is a hothouse for growing in wisdom. How do we respond to the demanding boss? How do we treat the difficult coworker? How do we exercise fairness in business? We need winsome wisdom! When I find myself in a sticky situation, an arrow prayer asking God for clarity and assistance helps me to pause and collect my thoughts before I blurt out something I will regret later.

Over the years, I've watched people come to my dad for wise counsel, particularly during his tenure as a professor at Taylor University. Colleagues and students alike came to him, seeking his advice on how to handle a challenging situation or relationship. My dad listened, a lot. He wasn't quick to give advice or solve the problem. He asked questions. His responses were seasoned with grace and truth. Even today, in their retirement years, others seek out my dad, and my mom, to talk things over and ask questions. Their combined life experience and years of deep faith have made them wise. In his early days at Taylor, Dad wouldn't have been such a "go to" guy because acquiring wisdom takes time. Wisdom develops out of spending time in God's Word and seeking his presence in the day-to-day matters of life. At work, whether we realize it or not, others do pay attention to our thoughtful response, our winsome reply.

For those who do not work in a Christian environment, Paul's admonishment to the Colossians is completely applicable today: "be wise in the way you act toward outsiders" (4:5 NIV). Do my colleagues feel comfortable or defensive around me? I myself have cringed listening to a Christian coworker insist on pointing out a tenet of the faith in every situation. When a work file is misplaced and later found, the fitting response is probably not, "God told me where it was." I am not suggesting that the habit of thanking God for his help in daily matters both great and small is not appropriate. I am suggesting that our faith in God can appear frivolous or insincere when we try too hard to mention him in every conversation. Paul's admonition to believers about how to act genuinely is helpful: "let your speech always be gracious, seasoned with salt" (Col. 4:6).

A parent once asked me if I really believed the faith statement of the school where I taught. While a faculty criterion required we be professing believers, the students themselves represented a variety of faith backgrounds or none at all. Her question, in all honesty, caught me off guard. After quickly asking God for wisdom, I told her "Yes, I do believe what the school stands for and so do all the faculty here." I had discerned what she was *really* asking in that moment. She wasn't wondering if God is real or if Christianity is true. She wasn't looking for a defense of the Gospel. She wondered whether or not the individual faculty members aligned with the same beliefs as the school. I kept my answer short and to the point, using "salt" sparingly.

WAYS TO ENCOUNTER GOD IN THE WORKPLACE

Whether you are sitting at a desk, or standing next to a patient, or driving in a car, encountering God's presence at work is no different than encountering him at home or anywhere else. No shift in mindset is required. It is another wonderful opportunity to experience God always *with* us.

BEGIN THE DAY WITH A PRAYER

I have built and maintain the habit of beginning my day with a simple prayer, inviting God's presence into my work and requesting his guidance. I do this while still lying in bed, or sometimes during my morning Bible reading. This small practice of invitation and request acknowledges Christ's lordship over all I do and begins my day with humility, as I recognize and acknowledge my need and dependence on God for wisdom in my work.

WORKPLACE COMMUNITY

Connecting with fellow believers during the workday is another way to experience God's presence. Workplace Bible studies or prayer groups can fit in before, during, or after work. In the chapter "Encountering God when Spiritually Adrift" I mention prayer times with my friend, Margaret. Sometimes we made a point of packing our lunches and eating together in an empty classroom; we connected in the middle of our day to chat over events and pray together. Sometimes we did this after school. Participating in a Bible study at the end of the school day has sometimes been efficient for me, making it easier on my evening schedule, rather than heading out after dinner for yet another commitment. Of course, we don't require a formal study or a set time to be an encouragement to each other. Pausing to listen to a colleague share a struggle and offering a reminder of our hope in God can happen *anytime*. Praying with a coworker in the moment can be more timely than struggling to find a time to meet later. These brief encounters where God's loving care for us and others is front and center refresh and strengthen us, and spur us on to run with perseverance the race marked out for us *today*.

And what about our non-Christian coworkers? Is it possible to connect with those who might secretly pigeonhole us as "a religious person" or who would be shocked to know we are praying for them to meet Christ? Of course it is. As a rookie 8th grade teacher, I struggled with whether or not to attend that Happy Hour I was invited to by my fellow teachers. Me hanging out in the Stagecoach Bar on a Friday afternoon didn't sound like a particularly effective witness. Thanks to the encouragement of my husband, who convinced me I *should* go, and along with another Christian friend, I enjoyed the relaxed festivities numerous times. During my teaching tenure in Waco, gathering after school for chips and queso and margaritas with my colleagues developed friendships and created memories. We talked, laughed, and shared life together. I know not every Happy Hour is tame; use wisdom and discretion to know when to accept an invitation and when to bow out.

Many social opportunities develop out of working together. The genesis of one of the first book clubs I attended was a workplace connection, and we ended up on outings to the theatre together, too. Spending time with colleagues away from work allows surface friendships to go deeper and provides the time and space for all sorts of conversations. We thank God for our workplace relationships and trust him to accomplish his kingdom work in them.

CELEBRATE THE SUCCESSES

Recognizing and celebrating the successes and joys of life are another way to encounter God in the workplace. We live in a culture quick to find fault, quick to criticize, and quick to say, "I told you so." Taking the time to congratulate a fellow manager for completing the project before deadline and under budget or celebrating a company milestone brings joy, meaning, and *esprit de corps* to our workplace. When a colleague is recognized for outstanding work, we are the first ones to offer our heartfelt agreement. And when a team member says, "I'm getting married!" we celebrate. When a coworker announces, "I'm pregnant!" we rejoice. Upon learning I had a publisher for this book, I sent an email to my colleagues telling them my good news. Instantly, congratulations flooded my inbox. The kind words confirmed they believed the publisher's decision to be a sound one—I *can* write a book! As Christians, our ability and willingness to come alongside our coworkers, to genuinely celebrate them and their accomplishments, reflects God's delight in the lives of his people.

SERVE OTHERS

Serving those we work side by side with loudly proclaims God's kingdom. Picking up the slack for a sick colleague will cost you: a longer workday, less time devoted to your own projects, or turning down a new client and the related pay bonus. But what a powerful way to demonstrate care, love, and Christ-likeness to a coworker. Nothing strikes panic into my heart faster than to be unexpectedly sick and forced to craft an easy lesson plan for a substitute teacher. On the few occasions this has happened, the gratefulness I feel when a fellow teacher says "don't worry, I've got your classes covered," is *beyond* words. Small acts of service are also huge. Refilling the photocopier with paper instead of walking away and leaving it empty for the next person; replacing the coffee creamer carton in the break-room refrigerator; inviting a colleague out to lunch after a trying work patch; bringing in a simple bouquet of flowers or favorite cookies for your assistant, "just because," when she or he has gone the extra mile for you once again—these are uncomplicated yet meaningful demonstrations of your awareness and consideration of others.

The last several winters on Long Island have been rough. Nor'easters and blizzards have dumped large snowfalls on us. After one delayed start to the school day, I entered my classroom to find water running down the walls in one corner. A pipe had frozen, blocking the melting snow from running off outside the building. And, horribly, it was the corner where I stored many of my books and student work! Dismayed, I grabbed towels and started to clean the mess before my students arrived. A colleague happened to be walking down the hall. Seeing the muddled, damp untidiness, she instantly started to help. Appreciation filled my heart. To be honest, if the tables were turned, I'm not sure I would have jumped in to help as quickly. I may well have begged off, using the "I have to get ready to teach" excuse. Cheryl's generosity has stuck with me. Her calm demeanor and willingness to set aside her own agenda modeled true service. When we serve our colleagues, we move beyond ourselves, exhibiting Christ-like behavior.

Recently, on a Christmas trip to my parent's house in Indiana, our driving route took us through Van Wert and past that very same Pizza Hut. Trying to catch a glimpse inside the windows, I wondered if any of "my crew" still worked there. I wish I could tell Sue the impact she made on my work ethic. She taught me well. I learned how to take accurate orders, how to make small talk, and how to correct mistakes. No matter where we work or what we do, God's presence goes with us. We show his kindness and wisdom, and offer our servant's heart to all who cross our path.

FOR FURTHER REFLECTION

1. What is the best part of your job? Why? If you could change one part of your job what would it be? Why? What steps can you take to make this change?
2. Spend some time thinking about your relationships at work. How well do you know your colleagues? How well does your workplace celebrate others and their accomplishments? How often do you see coworkers serving one another? Are there any ways you could influence your workplace environment in this regard?
3. What hinders you from connecting with God at work? In addition to my suggestions, what else would help to remind you of God's presence throughout your workday?

RECOMMENDED RESOURCES

Finding Livelihood: A Progress of Work and Leisure, Nancy Nordenson—Nancy's writing and observations gives voice to some of the thoughts and questions rolling around in my own head. *What constitutes good work? What is the difference between vocation and livelihood? Is there a difference?* Nancy states, "This book admits that work, even good work for which we are grateful and love, has a shadow side. It is not about disengaging from unsatisfying work or finding a new job. Instead, this book is about developing openness to meaning and beholding meaning where you find it. This book is about watching for signs of transcendent reality and participating in that reality, even when work fails to satisfy." From beautifully crafted sentences to rich vocabulary to honestly sharing about the failures and disappointments in her own life, Nancy weaves together a collection of essays that reflect truth, beauty and goodness.

Visions of Vocation: Common Grace for the Common Good, Steven Garber—Steven Garber is a friend of Ransom Fellowship, a ministry devoted to helping Christians think with discernment and started by Denis and Margie Haack. Steven's work receives high praise from the Haacks. This book is for anyone who wants to discover why vocation, or work, is good and explores ways we can flourish in our work as well.

Every Good Endeavor: Connecting Your Work to God's Work, Tim Keller—Now that we've moved close to New York City and are attending Redeemer Presbyterian on several occasions, the name Tim Keller carries some weight. Tim has the amazing ability to connect any part of life to the larger story of God's kingdom. Here he does this with the topic of work.

Work Matters: Connecting Sunday Worship to Monday Work, Tom Nelson—If you have ever struggled to connect your weekend to your work week, this book provides a theological perspective as well some practical help.

Work Matters: Lessons from Scripture, R. Paul Stevens—I had the privilege to hear Paul Stevens speak at Regent College on a number of occasions. The workplace was his specialty. This book gives a theological understanding about why work is important through the lens of Scripture.

Encountering God in Community

> The physical presence of other Christians is a source of incomparable joy and strength to the believer.
> —Dietrich Bonhoeffer, *Life Together*[37]

For four years, two Friday nights out of every month, eight of us gathered in our living room. We celebrated new jobs, new babies, milestone birthdays, and answers to prayer. We mourned the loss of loved ones, career setbacks, and strained family relationships. We played together too. One fall day we gathered at a local park to play touch football. After the game, we headed to another member's home to make pizzas and watch football on television. Memories such as these confirm to me the blessings of sharing life with others. Barring sickness or something unexpected, this small group was a protected time, a firm commitment, and each member showed up on our doorstep at 7 p.m. Our group consisted of four couples—Colby and Tammy, Rich and Tara, Tim and Carol, Brad and myself. How we found each other is a miracle in its own right, since all of us attended Willow Creek

Community Church in South Barrington, Illinois—a very *large* church, as many of you will know. During our time at Willow, the church started a ministry specifically designed for twenty-somethings. Through this ministry and a few other circuitous routes, we remarkably met each other and eventually formed a small group. This was a rich season in my life. Small group was a safe place to be myself. I belonged. These people knew me, shortcomings and all.

Community has played a prominent role in my life. Who I am as a person today has been shaped by my small-group experiences. Let me readily acknowledge that my participation in small groups significantly colors my sense of community. Within the context of group life, I have experienced the "mixed bag" of walking alongside others—the lovely, a bit messy, sometimes chaotic, even draining at times, parts of small-group life. But small group isn't the only type of community. Some of you don't belong to any "formal" type of group, yet you experience regular community with others. You live next to four or five other families and share life together by looking out for each others' houses, yards, or children. You celebrate holidays together and loan each other tools. Yet others of you belong to a fitness class or an art class and share a common goal or interest with those like-minded folks. Others of you attend churches that are too small to support a small-group ministry. Maybe you're part of a Sunday School class of 15-20 people, which serves as your community group. While many of the examples I share in this chapter draw from my small-group background, I believe a good deal of my observations and experiences are not unique. The truths outlined in this chapter are applicable in many community contexts. Whenever we share our lives with others, we welcome tangible aspects of God's presence among us.

We discover truths about ourselves and the kingdom of God.

WHAT IS COMMUNITY?

Psalm 133:1 begins, "How good and pleasant it is when God's people live together in unity" (NIV)! In the New Testament, we witness a young church practicing community. "And they devoted themselves to the apostles' teaching and the fellowship, to the breaking of bread and the prayers. And all who believed were together and had all things in common" (Acts 2:42, 44). These verses point to a fundamental component of community—the sharing of common values, interests, and attitudes. Part of what it means to be human is a desire to be known by others. God created us to be in relationships.

I teach the narrative poem "The Rime of the Ancient Mariner" by Samuel Taylor Coleridge to my seventh graders. A significant portion of the poem involves the Mariner's stages of penance for his heinous act of killing the albatross. In one heart-wrenching scene, the Mariner cries out, "Alone, alone, all, all, alone."[38] Not only must the Mariner suffer for his actions, but he must also endure his suffering alone. I tell my students that to understand the Mariner's pain, they must imagine (or remember) a time when they were really sick. Then they must imagine being really sick *and* completely alone. Nothing is worse than to feel miserable *and* to not experience the presence of one caring person. No tender hand reaching out to touch you, no one bringing you a cool drink, and no one gently tucking a blanket around you. My students totally understand this. I see it in their eyes: they nod their heads, they grasp the total awfulness the Mariner endures.

When I consider this earthly life, the condition of walking through it *alone* is one of the worst possible dooms imaginable, if not *the* worst. Even the most die-hard introverted, independent, I'm-Doing-It-My-Way person needs at least one friend, someone who shares interests and values. Sharing life with others is a way to know that we are *not* alone; to grow with others in the body of Christ; to experience God's grace in our daily lives. Consider the life of Jesus. When he began his earthly ministry, he gathered 12 men to walk alongside him. Even in a small group of that size, three of those men were especially close to Jesus. This example of community is a model for us. We need people in our lives who can speak truth to us; who can encourage us when we are discouraged; who can challenge us to pursue our God-given gifts.

How this community piece looks for each of us varies greatly. When we lived in the Chicago area, a favorite summer activity was to pack a picnic and head to Ravinia for a night of music in a lovely setting. Though there was ticketed seating, most people found spots on the lawn and listened to fantastic music, everything from well-known artists, to the Chicago Symphony Orchestra, to some up-and-coming artists no one had heard of yet. The people-watching side of me loved this event. Some people packed elaborate picnics, complete with candelabras, flowers, and small tables. Others stopped by the local gourmet grocery store, filling their take-out cartons with a gastronomical feast. Soon the lawn would fill and you would be surrounded by other picnickers. I loved hearing some of the stories shared before the concert started. As I listened, I heard snippets of how attending Ravinia with neighbors or a certain set of friends was a tradition. This is what they did every summer or every weekend night. They shared the responsibility of bringing food or finding the right place to sit. If I would have asked them, "Are you a community group?" they would have thought me crazy. Yet, as they gathered together to share common interests—good food and good music—community happened. The sharing of life occurred on the lawns of a northwest Chicago suburb.

While hanging out at Ravinia illustrates an informal, organic way to experience community, others seek a formal group. Individuals come together around shared interests, goals, or outcomes—gardening, Bible study, sewing, scrapbooking, or community theatre and with criteria based on gender, marital status, age, profession, and so on, ad infinitum. And some community contexts are not formal groups at all, but rather a less-or-more regular gathering of two to twenty-two people.

Since high school, my involvement in various Bible studies and discipleship groups has been fairly consistent. I have a strong memory of my college Discipleship Coordinator group. During my sophomore year, I served as the "DC" for my dorm wing, with the responsibility to nurture the spiritual life of the young women living on my floor. Every other week, all the DCs in English Hall met with the head DC for our own discipleship. For a few hours on Monday night, Crystal's room became a haven as we shared prayer requests and offered encouragement to one another. Over time, a deep bond formed among us. I cared about the women in this group and they cared about me. What started out as a requirement for my DC role—attend discipleship group—became much more than a "have to." Our common values and interests prepared the soil from which deep fellowship sprang.

WHY IS COMMUNITY IMPORTANT?

Isn't it remarkable that Jesus Christ came to earth in bodily form? As God of the universe, he could have revealed himself in a variety of ways. He didn't have to come as a baby and live a human life. But he did. It is so encouraging that he "gets" what my life is like through his own first-hand experience. It is also remarkable that one of the first things Jesus accomplished in his public ministry was to deliberately gather together a group of disciples. He formed the first community group! Over the next three years, these men would talk, travel, eat, sleep, and minister with Jesus. The disciples needed the physical presence of Jesus to teach and prepare them for the work they would continue to do once he returned to heaven. The times of fellowship and instruction would sustain these men as they faced persecution and for some, martyrdom. In our own lives, we need the physical presence of friends, mentors, associates, kindred spirits, coaches, and teachers too. As we experience the joys and sorrows of this life, celebrating and mourning with others, we model the type of community Jesus himself lived out while he was here on earth.

TO SERVE AND TO BE SERVED

Living life in community allows us to serve others and to be served; again, as Jesus himself lived out. The past several summers at Stony Brook, I have witnessed many examples of service within our community. As faculty come and go, a number of moves happen during the summer months. Each time, I marvel at how individuals give of their time and energy to load trucks or unload them. We also offer to help paint each others' houses or apartments, babysit young children, or provide meals. One of the common refrains from those who are new here is how blessed they feel to be a part of this community. We aren't a perfect community by any means, but our acts of service communicate love, care, respect, and welcome.

In one of the final moments with his disciples, Jesus serves his friends by washing their feet. It is easy to read this passage in the book of John and forget the details. Foot washing under the best of circumstances is not a glamorous task. In the ancient world, where sandals were *the* footwear, a person's feet were exposed to dirt all day long and antibacterial soap wasn't on offer. I have participated in foot-washing services. I always feel a bit awkward and uncertain as I wash another person's feet. What if her feet are dirty? What if his feet are smelly? Do I wash gently or do I scrub hard? The very act of kneeling in front of a person is also humbling. As Jesus approaches Peter, he objects. "No," said Peter, "you shall never wash my feet" (John 13:8). Yet Jesus insists and tells Peter that unless he does this, Peter will have no part with him. Jesus explains to his disciples *why* he did this. "If I then, your Lord and Teacher, have washed your feet, you also ought to wash one another's feet" (v. 14). Jesus' instruction to his disciples is for all who call Jesus Lord—*serve* others. Jesus also allows himself to *be* served. In John 12, Mary, the sister of Martha and Lazarus, pours expensive perfume over Jesus' feet, upsetting Judas Iscariot who thinks the perfume should have been sold and the money given to the poor. John, rather pointedly, states that Judas' concern did not stem from caring about the poor, but rather, the lost opportunity to pilfer some of the money from the sale of the perfume. Jesus rebukes Judas and tells him to leave Mary alone. What she has done for Jesus is important—she has served him. For some of us, it is easy to serve others, but much harder to allow others to serve us. Perhaps the equation is flipped. You readily accept the help of others, but rarely offer a helping hand yourself. We grow and learn when we do both—serve and be served. Participating in community provides these opportunities.

ATTENDING CHURCH ISN'T ENOUGH

You may think weekly church attendance meets your "community" quota, especially if you attend adult Sunday School. You talk with others before Sunday School, during Sunday School, before church, and after church during coffee hour. By the time you come home from church, you are talked out! But aren't most of those conversations social and superficial? How deep can you go standing in a crowded room with other church folk mingling within earshot?

One way we can go deeper is through service. Serving alongside others, over the long haul, week after week, month after month, year after year, forms deep relationships. Perhaps this is teaching the same Sunday School class with a friend, or serving a meal at a local shelter with a regular group of people, or cleaning the church with the same team every month. As I mentioned in my workplace chapter, we experience community, and Christ's presence, when we work and serve together. A deep sense of belonging develops when we serve in the same place. This can also happen when we circle together with the same faces week in and week out, joining our lives. During the first two years living in Waco, Brad and I joined a life group at our church. It was one of the first steps we took to make this new church our home. The Hoffmans, our life group leaders, exuded warmth and hospitality, hosting in their spacious home this large group, a mix of couples and singles representing all life stages. Just as we initially connected with this group, a couple recommenced attending after a prolonged absence, having recently lost an adult child to illness. Their grief was fresh and raw. This was the first time we were up close on a weekly basis with two grieving people. While Brad and I had experienced the tragic family death of Wendy, Brad's brother's wife, we didn't live close by; we had been shielded from witnessing much of his grieving, and our own grieving was likewise shielded from view. But in Waco, we had the privilege of observing over many months the anguish and affliction of loss for this couple. When the wife came to life group still in her pajamas, we knew it had been one of the hard days for her. Brad and I were never intimate friends with this couple, but I will always be grateful that they allowed us to enter into their journey of sorrow and distress. Sitting a couple of pews behind them in church or seeing them in the Fellowship Hall for coffee hour were *not* opportunities to learn from them and to care for them. While church attendance *does* provide important communal elements—we worship God together as a body of believers and we break bread together—there is a special kind of nurturing in a small group, where we can be ourselves, drop our guard, and allow others to witness our good days and our bad days.

LEARNING TO LOVE THE DIFFICULT PERSON

A group where everyone gels together well is the best case scenario. (This is true in any context where multiple people and personalities are involved.) You may be thinking, "I hope this group lasts forever!" But a group like that is rare. Prepare to be stretched! We expect that there will be one or two individuals who rub us the wrong way or who dominate the discussion. You start asking yourself, "is this group worth my time and energy?" Only you can decide if your group will work over the long haul, but don't bow out at the first sign of difficulty. Sometimes these are the kinds of situations where we learn to set healthy boundaries or we learn to speak honestly to others. I remember one such situation in my own life. It started with meeting a woman I'll call Karen. I first met her in a Sunday School class. She was new to the area and eager to become involved in church and community life. Once, our family invited her to join us for dinner at a local restaurant. Soon after this, my phone started ringing with requests for favors. I *did* want to help Karen, but I was becoming nervous. The requests were frequent. I had young children and not much flexibility. The tipping point hit when I came home after an afternoon of helping Karen to prepare for soon-arriving dinner guests. My phone rang. Karen needed more help. I told her I was unable to come due to my own dinner plans. The tearful begging that ensued was almost too much to bear. With great difficulty, and feeling like *the* biggest Christian failure *ever*, I gently but firmly told her the obvious: she needed to call someone else. Gathering my last ounce of resolve, I repeated that I couldn't help her in this instance and hung up the phone, racked with guilt. Karen never called me again. I later learned she moved back to her hometown. I also learned that my experience was not unique. Karen's repeated insistent, urgent demands for help pushed others away rather than drawing them closer. This is the messy, draining side of community life. I wanted to be the loving hands and feet of Jesus, but I also needed to set boundaries with Karen; I wasn't endlessly immediately available. Learning when and how to say "no," without strapping on the burden of unnecessary guilt, was an important lesson to learn. One I am still learning. Perhaps in your small group you have a too-talkative member. Finding ways to gently redirect the conversation, or to invite others to share, or even speaking directly with "Chatty Cathy" privately, may stretch you in uncomfortable ways.

Perhaps you are the too-talkative member. Do you walk

away from situations realizing you did most of the talking? Has anyone ever implied or told you directly that you speak too often? If you find yourself squirming just a bit and thinking this might describe you, pay attention to the relational dynamics the next time you gather with your friends or community. Look at each person and ask yourself, "Have I asked so-and-so a question about his or her life recently?" Learn to self-monitor. If you find yourself being the first to respond every time a question is asked or the one doing most of the talking, be silent for a while and allow others to share and talk. Spend some time reflecting on why you feel the need to respond to every comment or question. Ask a trustworthy friend who is a part of your community to let you know when you speak too much or dominate a discussion. This side of heaven, our sinful selves are part of the community mix. Sometimes, in our desire to share an important insight or tell a great story, we come off as insensitive or as a know-it-all. What a rich blessing to cultivate together the fruit of the Spirit, to have the opportunity to ask for forgiveness, to be intimately united in Christ with those who were once strangers and unknown to us, to witness up close the transforming work of God in someone's life or in our own life!

WAYS TO ENCOUNTER GOD IN COMMUNITY

More than once, just when I started to wonder "is this group a good fit for me or not," someone suddenly shared struggles or offered insights almost identical to my own current battles or thoughts. In that instant, a recognition and a bond formed that I can only attribute to God. "You mean you were feeling that way too?" This is one of the gifts of community;

a wonderful realization that we are not alone in our experiences or ideas. God's active presence is among us, drawing us to himself and to others. Encountering God in community embodies much of what we long for as human beings: the physical presence of another person in our lives; someone with real hands and feet; someone who can speak words of hope and comfort. Experiencing God in community requires mindfulness and attentiveness. It also requires our openness.

BE OPEN TO COMMUNITY

The older I become and the more individuals I meet, the more I marvel at the variety of personalities God created. When I first took the Myer-Briggs Type Indicator (a personality test) as a college student, I landed firmly on the extrovert spectrum of the scale. I have since moved to the middle, with score results equally straddling both sides of the equation. Some of this move to the middle may be due to the demands of my profession as a teacher. I told you about the small group Brad and I belonged to with three other couples at the beginning of this chapter. We all took the Myer-Briggs test together to help us understand each other better. The introverts tipped the scale in that group. In my late twenties then, I learned a lot from these more inward-looking friends. As incredible as it seemed to me, for some of them it was a stretch to be a part of this group (or any group). Sharing their lives with others exhausted them on one level. Too many small group activities drained them. Nonetheless they were committed to the group and knew they benefited from it, along with the rest of us. A particular highlight of our time was telling, as we affectionately titled it, "Who Is Me?" stories. Over the course of several months, we each presented our life story. Some used props.

Some brought photos. Some played music. Each one's story handed us important pieces of their personal puzzle that otherwise would have taken us years to know. God's hand of providence and sovereignty was observable in each "Who Is Me?" account. Not only did we affirm the storyteller for her life narrative to date, but we also thanked God for the different ways he had been at work, and was working, in her story. If you have excused yourself from small-group involvement because you are " not wired that way," please reconsider. Yes, there may be seasons where it is impossible to participate in a group. But don't make it a permanent season. Experience the ways God can use others to teach you about not just yourself but himself as well.

SHARING LIFE IN COMMUNITY

Just as reading quality literature mirrors real life, so too authentic community mirrors real life. When we eat, work, play, and pray together, the pressure to present ourselves in the best light gradually falls away. We understand that we are loved and valued, despite our shortcomings. We admit our need for God's grace in our daily lives. We respond to the nudges of others to change and grow. Sharing our lives with others pushes us in necessary ways.

EAT MEALS TOGETHER

Almost every group I have been a part of involved food. Whether it was bringing a snack to share or hosting a potluck once a month, eating together is a fundamental part of group life. As I mentioned in my Hospitality chapter, sharing a meal has a sacramental quality. The food is a vehicle, a conduit for joys and struggles to be brought into the light. Looking into the faces of those gathered around a table, we are knit together with loving grace. "Sharing food creates the bonds and relationships that are essential to any community, and is simultaneously a celebration of the goodness and wholeness and marvelous nature of a world that can produce such good things, and of a God who is first the creator."[39] Brad and I met together with a group for a number of years in Waco, consisting of fellow Baylor graduate students, a Truett Seminary student, and Baylor professors. I looked forward to our monthly kids-included potlucks. On dinner nights, we started a little earlier than usual and each person contributed something to the meal. Sometimes we needed two tables to accommodate all the adults and the children. Before we ate, we gathered around the table, sometimes holding hands, and offered up a prayer of blessing over the food. We invited God to join us around the table as we tucked into the good food, laughed, and shared stories together. These potlucks turned an ordinary work night into something extraordinary. If food isn't part of your group time, consider adding it to the blend. Or if it's been snacks only, try out a potluck, with spouses and children included. The beauty of a potluck is the shared responsibility. No one person is stuck in the kitchen, doing all the prep.

WORK TOGETHER

Most groups I have belonged to originated out of my local church, meaning readily accessible opportunities to join in on service projects or mission events. My current situation is unique in that I live where I work. Those of us living in the school-owned homes share a special connection, with some of our houses right next door to each other. We see each other walking or riding our bicycles to campus. We see each other hustling to the sports' fields or walking between academic buildings. In the summer months, we gather for cookouts and long evenings around a firepit. When school is in session, we still gather socially but not as frequently. We work together as colleagues, yes, but we genuinely like each other as neighbors and friends. Seeing each other in the classroom and then again in the dining hall for dinner or in someone's home adds a communal aspect to our jobs. We see each other in both our best and worst moments. Time and again, this community has closed ranks around an individual or a family in a time of difficulty, offering prayer and meeting practical needs—covering classes, providing childcare, and bringing meals. My employment situation is not the norm, I realize that (and count my blessings). But even before coming to Stony Brook to work and live, gathering together to accomplish a task got things done efficiently and with joy. Whether it was helping with Vacation Bible School, herding kids at Backyard Bible Club, or going into the city to serve at a local mission, working together towards a shared goal fosters community. Seeing others use their gifts and abilities in different venues knit us together and develops a deeper appreciation for one another. After each experience, we spend time debriefing and sharing our individual stories of what happened, affirming and celebrating God's work in our own lives and in the lives of others.

PLAY TOGETHER

I am a "let's do this together" type of person. I love thinking about or planning fun activities for the people in my life. This is one of the gifts I contribute to whatever group I am in. "Since we all love Mexican food, let's plan a fiesta and bring our favorite dishes," or "Let's plan a girl's day out and go for high tea in the city." Which we actually did. We made a reservation at downtown Chicago's Drake Hotel, dressed up a bit, and drove into the city for high tea. I have a lovely picture of the four of us gathered around the table—a special time indeed. When we play together, we catch a glimpse of what the Westminster Catechism means when it says "to enjoy God forever."[40] Whether it is a birthday, a new job, or a new baby, celebrating together is a foretaste of heaven. If you feel stuck in a rut, call "time-out" and deliberately do something fun with someone else. I love it when I am unexpectedly surprised by someone I *thought* I knew, like the time the normally reserved, somewhat quiet friend suddenly revealed a funny, witty side to her personality. The rest of us around the table laughed and marveled at this "new person." Our play times don't need to be elaborate or costly; organizing a game night or taking turns watching each other's favorite movies are low-cost, easy-to-pull-off events. The "pause button" is pushed on our daily routines, we give thanks for these wonderful people we know, and our memory buckets are filled. We are reminded that God designed us as whole persons—physical, mental, emotional, and spiritual beings. Playing together brings us joy and illustrates another facet of being made in the image of God.

PRAY TOGETHER

I can still recall the sheepishness in her voice as she asked for prayer. Her neighbor's dogs barked incessantly, particularly early in the morning, waking up the rest of her family. Would we pray that the dogs wouldn't bark as much and that her family could get some decent sleep? We did. Over the next few weeks God answered that prayer in a somewhat surprising manner. An anonymous group member purchased a Petsafe Ultrasonic Bark Control for the family, which emits a harmless, yet annoying, high-pitched sound that only dogs can hear. The Bark Control restored peace and quiet to the early morning hours for this family and kept neighborhood relationships intact. Does this strike you as an odd prayer request? One of the most tangible ways that we experience God's presence in community is by praying for and with one another, even about dogs and neighbors. Scattered liberally throughout the Bible are stories of God's people coming together in prayer. Paul's words in 1 Thessalonians 5:17 ring true for us today, "pray continually." Whether it is to pray for a brother or sister in need or to offer thanksgiving for answered prayer, the group that prays together forges deep connections. I have felt God's presence most powerfully when in prayer with my fellow brothers and sisters in Christ. In the lifting up of our burdens and in the spoken and unspoken words, God's Spirit has been present.

On the flip side, I've been sometimes frustrated by small group prayer time. Depending on the group size and the personalities involved, the *requests* for prayer can leave little time for *actual* prayer. Or one person can dominate the prayer time by sharing too much and not leaving time for others to make their requests known. It can be efficient to split up a larger group into smaller units for prayer, with two or three people sharing requests and praying together. But praying as a large group united in Christ can also be wonderfully appropriate. Those who feel led to pray, do so, the prayers going up as an offering to God, a sweet fragrance before the very throne of God. In one women's group, we practiced guided prayer. The leader opened our time and invited us to share sentence prayers of thanksgiving or praise. After each brief prayer, we responded with, "Thanks be to God." As we moved into a time of confession or intercession, our responses would be, "Lord, have mercy," or "Come, Lord Jesus." In couples' groups, splitting occasionally along gender lines provides a safe place to share sensitive requests. The laying of hands on an individual or a couple dealing with a difficult situation or to offer a prayer of blessing is a powerful witness, as the Body of Christ agrees together that nothing is impossible with God (Luke 1:37).

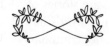

These days my Friday nights look different. I am often attending a school sporting event or simply crashing in front of the television—not preparing to host small group. The gift of that particular Friday night group fills me with fond memories and a foretaste of what is to come. When we participate in community, we catch glimmers of eternity where we will proclaim with all who call Jesus, Lord and Savior, "Look! God's dwelling place is now among the people, and he will dwell with them. They will be his people, and God himself will be with them and be their God" (Rev. 21:3 NIV). Until that day, may we hold fast to what we know is true. May we share the load of this life with others. May we proclaim with expectation, "Come, Lord Jesus."

FOR FURTHER REFLECTION

1. Make a list of all the ways you have experienced God's presence as a result of being in some type of community

group. Let this list serve as both an encouragement and a reminder of God's work in your own life and in the lives of your fellow members. If you have never been a part of a group, what are you waiting for?

2. What aspects of being in community make it difficult for you? Is there anything you can do to change or improve the situation?

3. If your group is in a rut, consider asking each group member to share his or her life story, taking several weeks or months to hear from everyone. You will be amazed at how much you learn! Your own faith will be encouraged as well.

RECOMMENDED RESOURCES

Lest Innocent Blood Be Shed, Philip Hallie—I received this book as a 40th birthday present. At first glance, you might wonder why I include this book here. This is the story of one French town during WWII, Le Chambon, that decided to save the life of every Jewish person (many of them children) who entered their village. Under the nose of the Vichy government, this community took great risks to hide and protect those most vulnerable. Community has the power to impart change and bring goodness and light in a time of darkness.

Life Together, Dietrich Bonhoffer—An excellent choice for a small group to study together. Bonhoffer's style is straightforward and practical. Readers will appreciate the way he portrays life in community. Using diverse examples, from scripture reading to singing to eating, this short book will inspire and challenge anyone seeking deeper Christian fellowship.

Critique, a publication of Ransom Fellowship (www.ransomfellowship.org)—I discovered Denis and Margie Haack at a L'Abri Conference in Rochester, MN, in the early 1990s. My life is richer and better as a result. They started Ransom to "help Christians develop discernment" particularly as it relates to popular culture. Don't go looking for Christian-only book, movie, and music reviews here! An oft-repeated phrase is, "We [Christians] live in Babylon," meaning we can't expect society to mirror Jerusalem just yet. Our Chicago small group used their discernment exercises as part of our study time. Many of these exercises center around issues that don't have a particular Scripture verse to reference. For instance, one case study dealt with a lesbian couple with two adopted children, living next door to a Christian family. A friendship develops between the two families. The lesbian couple asks for prayer and wants to have conversations about building their relationship and deepening family bonds. Eventually the topic of sharing babysitting comes up. What does Christian faithfulness look like in this situation? This type of question, and many more thought-provoking ones, are part of these discernment exercises. Good stuff for any group willing to wrestle with difficult, challenging questions.

Notes

Beginning

1   Edith Schaeffer, *The Hidden Art of Homemaking* (Wheaton, IL: Tyndale House, 1971), 31.

Chapter One

2   Gerard Manley Hopkins, "The Starlight Night", in *Hopkins: Poems and Prose* (New York, NY: Alfred A. Knopf, 1995), 24.

3   Loren and Mary Ruth Wilkinson, *Caring for Creation in Your Own Backyard* (Vancouver, BC: Regent College Publishing, 1992), 16.

4   Schaeffer, *Hidden Art*, 65.

5   Barbara Kingsolver, *Animal, Vegetable, Miracle* (New York, NY: Harper Collins, 2007), 186–89.

6   Carolyn Weber, *Holy is the Day* (Downers Grove, IL: Intervarsity Press, 2013), 126.

7   Isabella L. Bird, *A Lady's Life in the Rocky Mountains* (Norman, OK: University of Oklahoma Press, 1960).

8   Oswald Chambers, *The Discipline of Dejection* in *My Utmost for*

His Highest, (Westwood, OH: Barbour and Company, n.d), 27.

Chapter Two

9 Ray Bradbury, *Fahrenheit 451* (New York, NY: Simon and Schuster, 1951), 78–79.

10 St. Augustine, *On Christian Doctrine*, II.18.28.

11 Gladys Hunt, *Honey for a Woman's Heart* (Grand Rapids, MI: Zondervan, 2002), 33.

12 Linda Sue Park, *A Single Shard* (New York, NY: Yearling, Random House, 2001).

13 E. Annie Proulx, *The Shipping News* (New York, NY: Simon and Schuster, 1993), 1.

14 ———. *The Shipping News*, 336.

15 C.S.Lewis, *The Last Battle* (New York, NY: Collier Books, 1970), 184.

16 Romalda Bishop Spalding, T*he Writing Road to Reading*, ed. Mary E. North (New York, NY: Harper Collins, 2003), 122–23.

Chapter Three

17 Harper Lee, *To Kill a Mockingbird* (New York, NY: Grand Central Publishing, 1960), 32–34.

18 Timothy J. Keller, *Practicing the Christian Life*. "Hospitality." June 2008. MP3 sound recording.

19 Quoted in "Hospitality."

20 Julee Rosso and Shelia Lukins, *The Silver Palate Cookbook*, with Michael McLaughlin (New York, NY: Workman Publishing, 1982), 86.

Chapter Four

21 Sarah Orne Jewett and Mary Wilkins Freeman, *The Short Fiction*

of Sarah Orne Jewett and Mary Wilkins Freeman, ed. Barbara H. Solomon (New York, NY: Meridian Classic, 1987), 349–50.

22 *Merriam-Webster Online Dictionary* accessed June 14, 2016, www.merriam-webster.com/dictionary/ritual.

23 Susan Schaeffer Macaulay, *For the Children's Sake Foundations of Education for Home and School* (Wheaton, IL: Crossway Books, 1984), 80.

24 Jonni McCoy, *Miserly Moms Living On One Income in a Two Income Economy* 3rd ed. (Bloomington, IN: Bethany House Publishers, 2001), 114.

Chaper Five

25 C.S. Lewis, *The Screwtape Letters* Rev.ed. (New York, NY: Macmillan, 1982), 40, 42.

26 JRR Tolkien, *The Return of the King* (New York, NY: Ballantine Books, Random House, 1965).

27 Preston Yancey, *Tables in the Wilderness a Memoir of God Found, Lost, and Found Again* (Grand Rapids, MI: Zondervan, 2014), 28.

28 *The Expositor's Bible Commentary*, ed. Frank E. Gaebelien, vol. 6 Jeremiah, ed. Charles L. Feinberg (Grand Rapids, MI: Zondervan, Regency Reference Library,1986), 358.

Chapter Six

29 Andi Ashworth, *Real Love for Real Life The Art and Work of Caring* (Colorado Springs, CO: Waterbrook Press, Shaw Books, 2002), 1.

30 Doris Elizabeth Smith, age 93, went home to be with the Lord on June 24, 2016.

31 Anne-Marie Slaughter, "Why Women Still Can't Have It All," *The Atlantic*, July/August 2012.

32 Ashworth, *Real Love for Real Life*, 33–34.

33 Brother Lawrence, *The Practice of the Presence of God* (New Kensington, PA: Whitaker House, 1982). This is my phrasing but it captures the essence of brother Lawrence's writing throughout the book.

34 Edith Schaeffer, *With Love, Edith: The L'Abri Family Letters 1948–1960* (San Francisco, CA: Harper and Row, 1988) and *Dear Family: The L'Abri Family Letters 1961–1986* (San Francisco, CA: Harper and Row, 1989).

Chapter Seven

35 Lydia Saad, "The "40-Hour" Workweek Is Actually Longer—by Seven Hours," *Gallup.com*, Aug. 29, 2014, http://www.gallup.com/poll/175286/hour-workweek-actually-longer-seven-hours.aspx.

36 Lee, *To Kill a Mockingbird*, 39.

37 Dietrich Bonhoeffer, *Life Together The Classic Exploration of Christian Community*, trans. John W. Doberstein (New York, NY: Harper and Row, HarperOne, 1954), 19.

Chapter Eight

38 Samuel Taylor Coleridge, *The Rime of the Ancient Mariner* (New York, NY: Dover, 1970), 32.

39 Susan M. Felch and Gary D. Schmidt, eds., *The Emmaus Readers* (Brewster, MA: Paraclete Press, 2009), 8.

40 "Westminster Shorter Catechism Q.1," accessed Feb. 18, 2016, http://www.reformed.org/documents/wsc/index.html

ACKNOWLEDGMENTS

Good writing is the fruit of rewriting—sometimes a lot of rewriting! I have preached this to my students for years and now I have experienced it firsthand with this book. Two people kept this project alive when I wanted to quit and give up. Jacquelyn, your belief in me as a writer and the encouragement you gave in the form of emails and cards, along with your careful, time-consuming review of my manuscript, is sheer gift. This is a better book because of you. Brad, you cheered me on and believed I could do this from day one. You dreamed big for me even when I could not do it for myself. How grateful I am to share life with you!

Thank you, Jessica Snell, my editor for your thoughtful questions and helpful insights as I reworked sections of this book. It has been a pleasure to work with you! Thank you to the Kalos Press team for their work on this project: Lydia Tisdale, Robyn Clark, Julie Hollyday, Paige Landino, and Nathalia Kane. I am honored to call myself a Kalos author. Ed Cyzewski, thank you for your suggestions and insight in the early stages of this book. You helped me hone my voice as a writer. Gary Mar, your encouragement at a pivotal juncture in this project means the world to me. In case no one has told you, I think you have the spiritual gift of encouragement. Cara Dixon, I am grateful for the walks and talks we shared as you helped me sort out key sections of this book. Mom and Dad, so much of who I am has been shaped by your example and love. Thank you for your encouragement throughout this writing journey.

Edith Schaeffer, until we can enjoy High Tea together in heaven I am grateful for your books, which started me on this journey of encountering God in the everyday. Margie Haack, while most of our correspondence has been limited to email, I feel like I know you. How thankful I am for your writing, which continues to inspire and challenge me to see God in the ordinary.

My Stony Brook colleagues, some of you read early chapters of this book. Thank you for your gracious words and generous encouragement even though what you read was "rough."

To my past and present students: I am a better reader and writer because of each of you. Thank you for your encouragement and excitement about this book.

Finally, Jesus, my Lord and Savior. "To Him who sits on the throne, and to the Lamb, be praise and honor and glory and power forever and ever" (Rev. 5:13).

About Kalos Press

Kalos Press was established to give a voice to literary fiction, memoir, essays, poetry, devotional writing, and Christian reflection—works of excellent quality, outside of the mainstream Christian publishing industry.

We believe that good writing is beautiful in form and in function, and is capable of being an instrument of transformation. It is our hope and ambition that every title produced by Kalos Press will live up to this belief.

For more information about Kalos Press, *Everywhere God*, and/or our other titles, or for ordering information, visit us on our website: www.kalospress.org, or contact us by e-mail at info@kalospress.org

Digital Copies Of Encountering God

At Kalos Press, we've found that we often appreciate owning both print and digital editions of the books we read; perhaps you have found this as well. In our gratitude to you for purchasing a print version of this book, we are pleased to offer you free copies of the digital editions of *Encountering God*. To obtain one or more of these, simply visit the eStore of our parent ministry, Doulos Resources (estore.doulosresources.org) and enter the following discount code during checkout:

EncounteringDigital

If you purchased a digital edition, you may use the same discount code to receive a discount deducting the full price of your digital edition off of the purchase price for a print edition.

Thank you for your support!